HOW TO RESTORE FAITH IN THE WORLD'S PREMIER
LAW ENFORCEMENT AGENCY

WANTED

THE FBI
I ONCE KNEW

CHRISTOPHER M. PIEHOTA
FBI SPECIAL AGENT, RETIRED

Copyright © 2024 by Christopher M. Piehota
Executive Assistant Director (Retired)
Federal Bureau of Investigation

First Paperback Edition

All rights reserved. No part of this publication may be reproduced, distributed, or transmitted in any form or by any means, including photocopying, recording, or other electronic or mechanical methods, without the prior written permission of the publisher, except in the case of brief quotations embodied in critical reviews and certain other noncommercial uses permitted by copyright law. For permission requests, write to the publisher, addressed "Attention: Permissions Coordinator," at the address below.

Some names, businesses, places, events, locales, incidents, and identifying details inside this book have been changed to protect the privacy of individuals.

Published by Freiling Agency, LLC.

P.O. Box 1264
Warrenton, VA 20188

www.FreilingAgency.com

PB ISBN: 978-1-963701-06-7
E-book ISBN: 978-1-963701-07-4

DEDICATION

This book is dedicated to the special agents of the Federal Bureau of Investigation, past, present, and future, who have always made many personal sacrifices and who suffer sometimes painful experiences in doing what is right, for the right reasons, at the right times, to "protect the American people and to uphold the Constitution of the United States."

This book is also dedicated to my family, friends, colleagues, and mentors who made my FBI career possible. I would have tried to name you all individually, but I could not risk the chance of inadvertently leaving someone out. You know who you are, and I appreciate you more than you know.

Special gratitude to my wife, Lisa, who has been my best friend, stalwart life partner, and the best "national security wife" that anyone could ever hope for. She, more than anyone, deserves credit for this book. Throughout our lives together, she made me a better person and helped me to see past myself. Thank you for making everything good happen.

CONTENTS

Acronyms and Abbreviations ix
Preface xiii
Introduction xvii

Section I
An FBI Education: Learning, Leading, and Leaving

1   The Legendary FBI 3
     The FBI As an Icon 3
     The Influence of the FBI 4
     Proud Traditions 5
     Moving Forward 6

2   "Welcome to the FBI" 13
     Becoming an FBI Agent 13
     The Crime Fighting FBI 16
     Investigating a "New" Kind of Terrorism 17

3   How Things Work 23
     Newark Field Office 24
     Rules to Live By 26
     Practical Lessons 28

4   Getting a Training Agent 33
     New Agent Education 34
     Task Force Guidance 36
     Ownership and Outcomes 39

5   A Defining Moment for the FBI, the United States,
       and the World 45
     The Day That Changed Everything 45
     The Pre-9/11 Operating Environment 49
     Examination of Insufficient Efforts 50

6	Going to FBI Headquarters 55
	Moving Forward 55
	Forming Leadership Practices 56
	A New Assignment 59

7	Counterterrorism Division and a Transitioning FBIHQ 63
	The Impact of an Effective FBI Leader 64
	Leadership Preparation 66
	A Transitioning FBI 68
	Deprioritized and Demoralized 70

8	Getting By with a Little Help from My Friends 75
	SET and the New FBI 76
	A Groundwork for Challenges 78
	Observational Experience 81

9	Washington Field Office, Washington D.C. 87
	The Importance of Patience 87
	Learning to Lead Other Leaders 91
	Moving Forward 93

10	Terrorist Screening Center, National Security Branch 99
	Reporting for TSC Duty—A Somewhat Rude Awakening 99
	Learning from a Tough Leader—The Quick and the Dead 101
	Insights Learned 102

11	Special-Agent-in-Charge, Buffalo, New York, Field Office 107
	The Challenges of Being in Charge 108
	A Changing Culture 111
	Purpose and Mission Priority 116

12	Director, Terrorist Screening Center	123
	Directing the TSC	123
	A Broader View	127
	National-Level Issues, Great People, and Moving On	130
13	FBIHQ Executive Assistant Director—Science and Technology Branch	137
	Assessing Areas for Improvement—Another Cycle of Change	138
	People, Programs, and Systems	139
	Implementing Change, Yet Again	142
	The Value of New Leaders	144
14	Moving Toward the Last Mile	149
	Retirement	151
	Time to Do Something Else	156
	Finality	159

Section II
The Decline of the FBI: What Went Wrong?

15	Fidelity, Bravery, and Integrity—What Happened?	165
	Managing Cultural Challenge and Change	166
	The Marjory Stoneman Douglas High School Shooting	168
	Three Areas for Quick Assessment	171
16	The FBI's Handling of the Olympic Gymnast Sexual Abuse Case	177
	The DOJ-OIG's Review of the FBI's Handling of the Nassar Case	178
	Causal Inventory and Evaluation	181
	Applying the Three-Point Assessment to the Nassar Case	183

17 The Durham Report—Summary Assessment............191
    Crossfire Hurricane 191
    Crossfire Hurricane Discussion and Evaluation 194
    When All Was Said and Done.................................201

18 Cultural Changes and Effects on Leadership............203
    Post-9/11 Practices and the Impact to FBI
            Culture..203
    The Changing World of the Special Agent...............209
    Shifting Values 210
    Getting Credit..211

19 A New FBI Director and a New Way of Looking at
            Things..215
    Evolution or Devolution 216
    Introducing a Culture of Trepidation 219
    Social Perception and Appearances 224
    Operational Appearances..225

Section III
Moving the FBI Forward: Restoring Faith

20 How Does the FBI Move Ahead? 233
    The New Rules to Live By 233
    Ten Principles for Rebuilding the FBI....................236
    Embracing and Sustaining Change 244

21 Closing Thoughts 247
    Fostering a Climate of Honesty 248
    A Mandate for Strong Executive Leadership............249
    Mission Clarity and Reconnection..........................251
    Cultural Resurgence 251
    Last Words 252

ACRONYMS AND ABBREVIATIONS

FBI	Federal Bureau of Investigation
AD	Assistant director
AO	Administrative officer
ASAC	Assistant special agent in charge
ASC	Assistant section chief
BLM	Black Lives Matter
CHS	Confidential human source
CID	Criminal Investigative Division
CJIS	Criminal Justice Information Services
CTD	Counterterrorism Division
DD	Deputy director
DIOG	Domestic Investigations and Operations Guide
DOJ	Department of Justice
EAD	Executive assistant director
FBIHQ	FBI Headquarters
FISA	Foreign Surveillance Act
FISC	Foreign Intelligence Surveillance Court
IOS	Intelligence operations specialist
ISIS	Islamic State of Iraq and Syria
Lab	Laboratory Division
NCTC	National Counterterrorism Center
NSC	National Security Council
OGC	Office of General Counsel
OIG	Office of the Inspector General
Ops	Operations
OTD	Operational Technology Division
RA	Resident Agency

RPO	Resource Planning Office
SAC	Special agent in charge
SES	Senior executive service
SET	Strategic Execution Team
STB	Science and Technology Branch
SWAT	Special weapons and tactics
TA	Training agent
TRRS	Terrorism Reports and Requirements Section
TSC	Terrorist Screening Center
USIC	U.S. intelligence community
VCMO	Violent Crimes and Major Offenders
WFO	Washington, DC, Field Office

" It was always my goal to help the FBI accomplish its enduring national security and criminal investigative missions in the most effective and efficient ways possible."

PREFACE

I served nearly twenty-five years with the Federal Bureau of Investigation. At the time of my retirement in 2020, I was honored to serve in one of the organization's eight most senior career manager roles outside of the FBI director.

The FBI director is a political appointee who serves a ten-year term at the pleasure of the president of the United States. The next two levels of FBI career executive leadership are the deputy director and the associate deputy director. I served at the next level of leadership as one of the six executive assistant directors (EADs). The EADs led the six organizational branches that comprised the majority of FBI programs in a way similar to private sector C-suite executives. While I had the privilege of leading large enterprise functions as an EAD, I was also fortunate to serve in a variety of previous leadership and operations roles. As such, I was present for certain conversations, interesting circumstances, and historical decisions that influenced the FBI's evolution over the years. I was fortunate to know many people who were instrumental in shaping the bureau, for better or worse. Later in my career, I was even more fortunate to advance into senior organizational roles in which I developed and applied the lessons learned throughout my leadership, management, and operational experiences. As I learned from my valued mentors and others who showed me what practices to avoid as a leader, it was always my goal to help the FBI accomplish its enduring national security and criminal investigative missions in the most effective and efficient ways possible. I endeavored to facilitate a beneficial leadership and working environment wherever I could.

As I wrote this book, it was my hope that I had some measure of success in helping the highly capable people I was privileged to work with and for. I also hoped that I would help my team members by supporting them, protecting them from unearned scrutiny, solving problems, offering solutions, and being part of a productive and rewarding mission environment.

Thank you all for your mission dedication.

"I believe the FBI can recover and regain the trust, confidence, and faith of the American public."

INTRODUCTION

Today's FBI could benefit greatly from a return to the leadership models, cultural traits, and operational practices that made it great. To some degree, these factors were deprioritized, watered down, and sometimes discarded for new-era management approaches embraced by corporate America over the past decade or so. The gradual departure from what made the FBI iconic became a procession of short-term and strategic errors, the results of which would not be clear for years to come. The FBI, at its soul, is not comparable to Silicon Valley technological organizations; nor is it similar in culture to banking, retail, or financial organizations. Yet the management practices of these types of private sector organizations were benchmarked by FBI senior leaders in the mid- to late-2000s, and then again circa 2014 to the present, in one fashion or another. These were then integrated or mandated into the bureau's cultural and operational environments. Starting with a cycle of cultural changes after the events of September 11, 2001, the FBI was transformed from a reactive crime fighting organization into a domestic intelligence and security organization. During this sometimes heavy-handed (and ham-handed) process, many of the organization's more tenured members became confused and disenfranchised. People with intermediate levels of tenure were mostly confused, and the newer members were simply looking for guidance on what to do. In the years following September 11, 2001, the FBI implemented many changes—some for the better, through significant investments and improvements to its technology and infrastructure. On the other hand, some changes planted the seeds for various problems and challenges that are eroding the FBI's standing with the American public. That said, I believe the FBI can recover and regain the trust, confidence, and faith of the American public. I am confident that a return to the FBI's previous stature can occur with an assertive return to proper mission dedication and operational focus on every level. This recovery will take humility and an unshakeable organizational will to do better and to be better in everything.

To make this recovery a reality, the FBI must have leaders who can conduct its mission without caving to political hedging, social engineering and spin doctoring, careerism, organizational distractions, and a weakening corporate character. Given an expedited return to a proper leadership environment and a laser focus on mission excellence, the people of the FBI can and will make things right. This return will also require an unshakeable will by our national leaders to place the right people in top leadership roles and to support them while they urgently create a renewed sense of mission, dedication, and obligation. Simply playing leadership musical chairs with the usual DC suspects will not garner the needed results. Our national leaders must realize that doing what has always been done will get us what we have already gotten—which we do not want anymore. Cosmetic changes and "happy talk" will not get the job done any more now than in the past. The FBI must redevelop and sustain the endurance and warriorship it once had to outlast political pressure and resist giving in to emotional influences. The FBI must do this while also protecting us from the national security threats and crime problems that face our nation. In addition, the FBI must embrace the short-term discomfort of being reset to once again fulfill the expectations of the country it serves.

Introduction

The American people deserve no less yet need much more from their FBI.

The people of the United States need the FBI, but we need it to be better led and more mission-focused rather than punished, contrite, and temporarily brought to heel. The FBI must return to its apolitical position within the DC political jungle. We need our FBI to be an objective, highly competent investigative organization that is free from political maneuvering or personal agendas. The word of the FBI was inviolable at one time and must become so again. The bureau must be willing to fundamentally change and possibly sacrifice itself and its own interests to become the trusted organization it had once been. The people of the United States will not see any benefit if the FBI behaves like just another chastised government agency. It cannot simply comply with sanctions that are levied upon it and then continue going about its business in mediocrity, dysfunction, or indifference.

The FBI must aggressively return to its sacred mission where it will be known again as objective, honest, and high performing as it "protects the American people and upholds the Constitution."

The FBI can and must do this.

The United States needs it.

The American people deserve it.

SECTION I

AN FBI EDUCATION: LEARNING, LEADING, AND LEAVING

"Principled, fearless leadership will be the key to future FBI success and the success of all organizations that do important things for the world."

1

THE LEGENDARY FBI

The Federal Bureau of Investigation is part of the United States Department of Justice. The FBI acronym is among the most well-known around the world. The organization was founded in 1908 to combat emergent crime problems created by new levels of societal wealth, increasing crime, and a new threat vector identified as the "automobile," which allowed criminals to travel more easily across state lines.

The FBI As an Icon

Possibly the most storied law enforcement organization in US history, the FBI has developed a certain mystique in popular culture and throughout the law-enforcement community. Its image evolved over the years from Elliott Ness and the *Untouchables* to Joe Friday of *Dragnet*, to Clarise Starling of the *Silence of the Lambs*, to Fox Mulder and Dana Scully of the *X-Files*, to the crime fighting team of *Criminal Minds*, to other prevailing forms of entertainment that featured the bureau and its storied past.

Various iterations of FBI-based movies, television shows, and books saw the bureau fill roles from heroes to villains to comic relief. Through them all, the FBI established a place in American culture that few other organizations can match. In its more official capacity outside of American popular culture, the FBI has also been a resolute protector of United States interests and the American public's safety since its inception and has achieved a host of remarkable accomplishments throughout its history. From World War I through the prohibition years and gangster years to modern-day national security threats and global crime problems, the FBI continually evolved to meet threats to our society.

The Influence of the FBI

The FBI made its way through World War II, the Civil Rights Movement, Vietnam, and the events of September 11, 2001, and it now finds itself engulfed in the intensifying political and social strife that impacts our nation.

The FBI has had its share of successes, but it has also run into various instances of shortfall, bad decision-making, and substandard performance in its evolution. We have to look no further than the circumstances surrounding how it investigated Dr. Martin Luther King, Jr., or its investigation of US citizens under the infamous COINTELPRO initiative to see how the mighty FBI could stumble. That said, the bureau is not and has never been a perfect organization, but it has enjoyed more wins than losses over the years. Nonetheless, today's FBI has been seen by some in the political and social arenas as struggling to maintain its objective mission focus, as well as its former trusted standing, as the "World's Premier Law Enforcement Agency."

This book will offer areas for discussion through my eyes regarding the FBI's journey from September 11, 2001, to the present. I will look at how the bureau changed in a few key areas, provide an expedited tour of some of my formative career experiences, and offer personal insights on what happened to the organization that once held the highest regard and trust of the nation it serves. I will close with some ideas on what might be done to realign its operations and spirit in a way that will inspire a return to expected levels of confidence, trust, and admiration.

Proud Traditions

Over the years, many people saw the FBI as an incorruptible, monolithic organization that represented the highest levels of honor, trustworthiness, and competence. Government agents in dark suits, the descendants of a lineage of achievement and lore, built the FBI's reputation into nearly mythical proportions. The projection of stoic professionalism from its special agents and professional staff members, as depicted in various movies and stories, filled the imaginations of many people with visions of seeking FBI careers and upholding the proud traditions and values that the bureau was built on. It was this same stoic professionalism that filled the hearts of criminals, spies, and terrorists with fear and dread in knowing that, if they were unfortunate enough to draw the FBI's attention, the FBI **would** find them, and they would be brought to justice.

As I moved through my career, I had the privilege to meet and work with people who properly represented the organization in terms of professionalism and performance and whose dedication helped to build the storied reputation of the bureau. However, I was also exposed to the realism of some of the organization's shortfalls and challenges that were previously concealed from the external view of mere mortals. Each exposure helped to frame my approach to becoming the best FBI special agent I could be. I worked closely with friends and colleagues to support the bureau's broad mission and honor its legacy. My colleagues and I had been granted the gift of becoming a part of FBI history, and I hoped to properly honor that gift.

Moving Forward

Please note that the following content is not intended to serve as a precise, all-inclusive recounting of FBI historical events (favorable or unfavorable in nature). The accounts in this book are based solely upon my experiences, personal observations, and professional interpretations of various circumstances and activities over the past couple of decades.

This book is not an attempt to cast undue praise or condemnation onto any specific persons in the situations I described. I did not intend this to be an all-inclusive report of FBI activities, and it should not be interpreted as such. Where applicable, I purposely avoided naming names, but I made reference to job titles, roles, or pseudonyms. I adopted this practice to protect the privacy and the personal security of my former colleagues, as well as their families or friends. If they choose to read this book, most of them will know who they are. In addition, I did not offer detailed instructions on how the FBI could upgrade, change, or rehabilitate itself to overcome some of the challenges it faces—that kind of assessment could follow in a separate document. Instead, I chose to offer more strategic observations in such areas.

I did not intend this book to be a recount of specific FBI operations and investigations. It is my personal recollection of some circumstances that impacted how the bureau moved toward its current stance in terms of its leadership, culture, and practices, and previously setting the standard for others to follow. I chose to avoid specific details in the interest of brevity, readability, and operational security, and in consideration of readers' endurance. I would be glad to engage in separate conversations focused on various details and factors of interest through separate discussion forums.

While this book looks at the FBI and its journey through my experiences, the organizational concepts and observations can be readily adapted to most any organization that struggles with its performance, effectiveness, and organizational culture.

Many of the examples I provide can apply to various other governmental agencies and private-sector organizations. The discussions on the impact of leadership and culture on an organization's performance cannot be overstated. Most problems that organizations face are likely the result of defective leadership practices and/or a deficient organizational culture. These defects and deficiencies can suppress the beneficial values, beliefs, and practices that sustain organizations through successes and shortfalls. History has shown us that the right leaders with the right attributes who are leading the right teams can accomplish almost anything. History has also shown us that bad leadership can derail even the most capable organizations from being successful.

At the time of this writing, the FBI has been subjected to bouts of withering critique on its priorities and practices. Serious questions have been posed about the bureau's political leanings based upon its internal intelligence reporting (leaked to the public) and its perceived treatment of people who are considered "more conservative." The organization's leadership environment has been strongly questioned in formal channels by official whistleblower testimonies and informally through the networks of active and retired FBI personnel. There have even been allegations of reductions in hiring standards and a deterioration in the quality of special agent recruits to fit organizational preferences under so-called "diversity, equity, and inclusion" goals. These types of revelations are devastating, and all of these matters spell trouble for what was once seen as the "World's Premier Law Enforcement Agency."

I was stupefied and sometimes horrified to hear these and other unflattering criticisms about what was once "my FBI." I have often wondered, "What happened?" I have tried to determine how the FBI got to this place. I am confident that many people across the US are asking these same questions or are thinking along similar lines. This is not the FBI that most people grew up with and trusted.

I am reminded of a conversation that I had circa 2019 with some executives from a top West Coast technology company. They asked, "What is going on with the FBI? What is going on in Washington, DC?" I thought for a few seconds and replied, "Do not worry about the FBI. It is going through some tough times, but it will be fine. Do not be distracted by the Washington, DC circus. The FBI that I know is the same FBI that protected your grandparents, your parents, and you as a child. This is the same FBI that will protect you, your children, and their children. The people of the FBI will not fail you."

I am not as confident in that statement now. That is why I chose to write this book. My objective is to relay my thoughts and experiences to reveal some of the causal factors I saw for some of the organization's challenges. I will provide insights on simple, but not easy, ways to reverse what could be seen as a possible organizational decline within our FBI.

The FBI has not been successful in resisting certain political and social factors that have led to the current state of affairs. Since the tragedy of September 11, 2001, the FBI has been forced to evolve, but it has not always properly kept its focus on what it should be and what it should be doing. Since that time, the bureau has worked to be faster in its activities but may not always have focused on being better. The FBI wanted to improve its use of technology, but it may have prioritized that course of action over the meaningful training and development of its culture and its people. The FBI mandated a change in its organizational culture after September 11, 2001, as a means of survival and may have done so at the expense of its soul. It wanted to become a "leadership factory" in the words of one FBI director. Instead, it focused on metrics, climate surveys, flowery new leadership approaches, and colorful slide deck presentations rather than prioritizing true applications of leadership and warriorship—both of which seem to have become elusive if not absent over time.

I will touch upon these and other points from the perspectives taught by the old breed of special agents who built the reputation of the FBI. To be fair, these special agents were not perfect; they were a mixture of saints and sinners and made their fair share of mistakes. What is important is that they were the protectors of the FBI faith that our country and its people once trusted and depended on. These old breed special agents were the dragonslayers that we all wished we could be. Their values and beliefs made the FBI what it once was and what it could be again. It will be through the lens of these values and beliefs that I offer my experiences.

Principled, fearless leadership will be the key to future FBI success and the success of all organizations that do important things for the world.

There are no bad regiments; there are only bad colonels.
(Napoleon Bonaparte)

FILE REVIEW

During my time with the FBI, I learned about the file review process. This process is the FBI's most basic, internal, investigative quality assurance process in which operations and investigations are given periodic critical supervisory review. These reviews assessed case agent performance in the areas of compliance with policies, investigative acumen, previous accomplishments, use of time and resources, administrative documentation, and execution of previous supervisory instruction.

File reviews were conducted approximately every ninety days (or more frequently if necessary) and served as an opportunity for supervisors to offer feedback, additional instructions, corrective counseling, and mentoring for investigative personnel.

Throughout the course of this book, you will find file review entries reflecting the lessons and mentoring provided to me from the old breed special agents who built and maintained the culture that made the FBI legendary. It is hoped that these reviews adequately highlight the various concepts that could help any organizational leader achieve their mission or purpose.

"The FBI had to change to engage this new adversary and the resultant threat environment that had become a frightening reality."

2

"WELCOME TO THE FBI"

Being a former active-duty member of the US Air Force, I was familiar with the concepts of command, control, and communication, and I had worked within clearly established hierarchies of rank and seniority. As such, I had no issues transitioning into the FBI business environment, which was more of a management system rather than the strict paramilitary rank structure favored by other law enforcement agencies and departments. Many of my new agent colleagues came from various backgrounds ranging from airline pilots to law enforcement officers to US Army rangers to lawyers to physical therapists. The management system the FBI adopted seemed to make sense in how to best manage such a diverse group of Type A people; however, I believe that this relaxed environment could have contributed to some of the inconsistencies in leadership approaches and declines in organizational discipline that I observed throughout my career.

Becoming an FBI Agent

Upon entering onto duty with the FBI in 1995, I reported to the FBI Academy in Quantico, Virginia, for basic new agent training; however, like most things, it was actually a bit more complicated.

In my pre-FBI life, I was working at the Kennedy Space Center in the Space Shuttle program, which had already reached its peak and was on the downhill side of its lifecycle. I worked for the Kennedy Space Center as a metrologist and provided scientific services in the field of quantification, measurement, and calibration. I would be glad to answer questions about metrology in a separate forum to save readers from a punishing discussion on platinum resistance thermometry, helium leak rate analysis, and microwave/optical power (among other technical operations I participated in).

I did not see myself outlasting the eventual demise of the Shuttle program, so I began exploring other career options. I had enjoyed my time with the US Air Force, and a return to military service was part of my career strategy. I was also interested in a career in law enforcement, and I began looking into and applying for related career opportunities.

I applied to the FBI through the Tampa Field Office in the mid-1990s, but I did not know that the bureau was just about to end a three-year hiring freeze due to previous federal budget reductions. After several months, an FBI hiring manager finally called on a Monday morning in July 1995 and asked if I was still interested in a career as a special agent. I replied that I was interested. The FBI hiring manager then asked if I could attend a class that was scheduled to begin on the upcoming Sunday. I responded that I could definitely make it. The caller then provided instructions over the phone on how to find the FBI Academy and advised me on how to check in to begin agent training. I thanked the manager and then set the phone down.

I had a lot to accomplish in a short time. I had to resign from my employment with the Kennedy Space Center, withdraw from the Florida Army National Guard Officer Candidate School that I was attending, pack for a sixteen-week separation from my wife and children, and make my way from Florida to the FBI Academy in Virginia by Saturday of that same week. Oh, I also had to tell my wife about the life decision I just made.

I told my wife what was going on, and she said, "Let's do it." She helped me to get ready, and we talked with our ten-year-old children about my being gone for a while (my wife and I were gifted with boy and girl fraternal twins). I closed out my personal logistical matters and professional administrative requirements at the Kennedy Space Center. I completed the necessary separation paperwork with the National Guard. I packed my car and got ready to drive from Florida to Virginia. Over the course of five days, I changed the course of my entire life, and I was going to become an FBI special agent. In line with true government efficiency, I received my formal employment acceptance letter about three weeks after my new agent class began: "Welcome to the FBI."

I will not belabor the FBI Academy experience here with a description of what I participated in because almost everything I did at the academy has been replaced or updated several times since my time there. But the FBI Academy was a good experience, and I appreciated all of the training and guidance we received. After a fun-filled sixteen weeks of classroom instruction, firearms training, physical training, defensive tactics, and other miscellaneous areas of instruction, I received my credentials from FBI Director Freeh and was a newly minted FBI special agent. After graduation, I reported to my first duty station at the FBI Newark Field Office in Newark, New Jersey.

At the FBI Academy and later at the Newark Field Office, I was welcomed to the bureau by senior special agents, the old breed, who served as formal and informal authority figures who had already earned their place with the FBI. These senior agents were the first line of conditioning that I received as I sought to earn a place in this storied organization. My first exposure to these agents was with those who served primarily as instructors and counselors who moved new agent classes through FBI Academy training cycles that would prepare us for our initial field office assignments. My next level of interaction with the old breed was through the senior agents in the field who provided our next phase of instruction and educated us on how to navigate the FBI and successfully function as special agents. Looking back, I am grateful for the time these old breed senior agents took to patiently explain how the organization worked, define who we should be as FBI special agents, instruct us on how our jobs should be done, and show us how to avoid the various pitfalls that could block one's way to a successful FBI career.

The Crime Fighting FBI

When I was beginning my FBI career in the mid-1990s, the bureau was seen by many people as the highest level in the law enforcement world. FBI special agents had a feared reputation among criminals as being some of the best manhunters and crime-solvers on the planet. The bureau was viewed as the best at certain crime fighting activities and operations (no disrespect intended for my fellow law enforcement brothers and sisters). The FBI rescued kidnapped parties, solved bank robberies, investigated public corruption matters, hunted down serial killers, and pursued a host of other reactive crime fighting activities. When an individual or group violated the applicable laws, it would result in a swift reaction from the FBI. Investigators would begin their work and would skillfully identify, locate, and apprehend applicable parties. FBI special agents would then present an air-tight case to federal prosecutors. Case closed.

Most new agents wanted to work in the FBI's reactive crime programs under the old Violent Crimes and Major Offenders

(VCMO) program umbrella. In this program, special agents often collaborated with other federal, state, and local partners to hunt down and arrest dangerous or high-profile criminals who drew the attention of federal law enforcement. The bureau also maintained warrant arrest squads, drug-related enforcement programs, and white-collar crime programs that often drew the attention of new agents who wanted to work in the FBI's top-tier criminal investigative world. I ended up in other areas of interest.

Investigating a "New" Kind of Terrorism

I entered into service with the FBI a couple of years after the 1993 bombing of the World Trade Center. This event sent ripples throughout the organization and severely taxed the law enforcement world in terms of what a proper response to an act of terrorism on US soil was or should have been. The FBI was excellent at reactive crime fighting, but the US had not yet been subjected to "modern" terrorism on our own soil. As a result, there was a fair amount of uncertainty about the application of available legal authorities and the need for new legal frameworks and investigative technologies to combat the scourge of terrorism.

The bureau found itself wrestling with the newly perceived importance of proactive operational analyses, predictive intelligence, information sharing, and focused threat prevention as foundational components in its operational models. Previously, the FBI relied heavily on the experience and skills of its special agents and the proven value of a programmed investigative reaction to breaking the law. Basically, the FBI and its partners were trying their best to fit the proverbial square national security peg into the historical round law enforcement hole to address what was an evolving threat environment. This exercise in futility was further complicated by historical tensions and cultural divides within and between the law enforcement and intelligence communities—which were not inclined to share information with each other. As another confounding factor, there was very little earnest operational coordination or collaboration between these communities, which would be talked about again with great energy shortly after September 2001.

Based on the first World Trade Center attack in 1993 and other overseas terror activities, I became interested in the phenomenon of terrorism and was assigned to the Newark field office's counterterrorism program (long before it was fashionable to work in national security programs). While I learned about counterterrorism investigative work, there were several more years of corporate head-scratching and turf battles while the FBI's counterterrorism program dealt with situations such as the Oklahoma City bombing (1995) and the Olympic Park bombing (1996).

While the FBI's view of international counterterrorism operations slowly matured, these terror events again rattled the organization, and we saw the emergence of a domestic terrorism threat picture. Various domestic extremist groups and militia movements began to gain prominence. The FBI defined domestic terrorism as "violent, criminal acts committed by individuals and/or groups to further ideological goals stemming from domestic influences, such as those of a political, religious, social, racial, or environmental nature." This "new" kind of terrorism (which was not really new, as it had evolved from similar activities in US history) gave the FBI a host of new challenges. The FBI found that the majority of people involved with domestic terrorism activities were US citizens and were entitled to free speech and other protections provided by the Constitution and other US legal frameworks. The FBI tentatively walked this Constitutional tightrope and created new programs and management structures for the emerging domestic terrorism threat. It then moved on to manage other competing national priorities.

While the FBI's domestic terrorism program was new and had the spotlight in the mid- to late-1990s, I was more interested in the phenomenon of international terrorism and worked mainly on these types of investigations. I was fortunate to work in investigative activities that exposed me to the finer points of human intelligence operations, surveillance techniques, technical collection, classified information handling, and geopolitics. I also worked with US intelligence community partners and collaborated with international security services. I learned how to work with other government agencies while I navigated the worlds of covert and clandestine operations. I enjoyed this line of work and applied myself to learn all that I could in how to detect and prevent acts of terrorism. I would find later that I would not be able to learn or do enough—soon enough.

As we moved toward the late 1990s, there was an unfortunate drift back to what was largely considered the "normal FBI business" of reactive crime fighting with a focus on violent crime, white-collar crime, public corruption, etc. Everyone moved back to the business as usual of bureaucracy, turf battles, complacency, and indifference to predictive threat analysis—all of which were seen by many, in retrospect, as contributing factors that eventually paved the way to the tragedy of September 11, 2001. The world changed on this date, and the FBI's culture, people, practices, and operational focus would never be the same.

After September 11, 2001, I was never the same. The FBI had been bested by a terrorist adversary that was different from any we had seen in the past. This new adversary, Al Qaeda (the Base), was led by a relatively unknown actor (at the time) named Osama bin Laden. This new adversary was not interested in ransom, hostages, or other previously seen terror practices. Members of Al Quada were willing to die to achieve their objectives. They had effective long-term planning and good execution and seemed to know how to evade our investigative efforts and static security measures. I knew I had to be better and do better, but this realization would not change what had happened on that September morning.

In hindsight, the FBI's investigative focus and legacy investigative protocols, circa the mid-to-late-1990s, were not good enough to detect and prevent the events on September 11, 2001. The Al Qaeda adversary was better than we were. As a result, innocent people lost their lives and others lost family members, loved ones, and friends. We knew that this kind of tragedy could never happen again. The FBI had to change to engage this new adversary and the resultant threat environment that had become a frightening reality.

FILE REVIEW

The FBI, like many high-functioning, highly successful organizations, had carved out its niche and had become the standard in crime fighting. In becoming the pinnacle of the law enforcement community, it also fell victim to a deadly organizational disease called complacency. The FBI did not use its imagination to look forward into the threat environment. Instead, it fell back on its past success and crime fighting prowess and found itself out-maneuvered by a dedicated, effective adversary.

According to Andy Grove, "Success breeds complacency. Complacency breeds failure." The FBI was beaten by an organization that had superior vision and execution. The lesson is that an accomplished organization that becomes complacent can and will be beaten by organizations that are agile, hungry, and motivated. The FBI did not focus on evolving threats and failed to see the operational horizon. The FBI did not allocate the required resources to be a strategic, learning organization that hunted for threats as opposed to reacting to threats.

Former US Navy Seal Jocko Willink has been credited with saying, "Complacency kills." He was correct, and thousands of people died on September 11, 2001.

"You can win battles and lose the war across the course of your career."

3

HOW THINGS WORK

Before I move further through my brief discussion on the events of September 11, 2001, I would like to take a step back to when my time with the FBI began and how it shaped much of the views, values, and practices that would guide the rest of my career.

I do not clearly remember my first few weeks of transitioning into the FBI's Newark Field Office from the FBI Academy in late fall of 1995. It was a blur of confusion and anxiety while I tried to figure out where I would fit in and how I would assimilate to this new working environment.

As noted earlier, a lot of people ask about the FBI Academy. What I tell them is that it was a good overall experience, and that the academy atmosphere was a mixture of community college with mandatory firearms training and gym class (albeit a gym class that included handcuffs and plastic guns). Most of the stress at the academy was self-induced through the fear of failure, threat of injury, or the fear of drawing an unfortunate first field office assignment.

Back then, we got together as a class toward the mid to latter part of the sixteen-week class training cycle so the instructors could have a good time seeing what office assignments were given to the students. During that festive evening, I drew the field office in Newark, New Jersey, which I figured was an unfortunate assignment due to the groans (and some sympathetic sighs) from my senior agent counselors. I tried to remain optimistic, and after the encouragement of my class counselors, I attempted to contact my identified Newark squad supervisor a few days later to discuss my new assignment. I called the Newark Field Office switchboard, reached the applicable squad secretary, and introduced myself. The secretary simply said that the squad supervisor was busy and then promptly hung up on me. Outstanding.

My wife cried when I told her where we were going, but she supported me as always. She quickly regained her sense of humor and adventure and started her parallel FBI career as my "national security wife." In this role, she skillfully began her navigation of what would be twenty-five years of managing my early mornings, late nights, weekend work, holiday call-outs, high-stress situations, and long hours required of FBI special agents. She did all of this in addition to her own doctoral studies, highly successful career in the field of education, and concurrent mission of being an exceptional mother to our two children (all of which she excelled in).

Newark Field Office

While I was still at the FBI Academy preparing to complete my time there, my wife started sending me newspaper clippings about Newark, New Jersey (of course, the Internet was not quite a thing back then). She highlighted that, at the time in the 1990s, Newark had the dubious honor of being very highly ranked in national statistics for (or infamous for) carjackings, AIDs cases, murder, general crime, lousy roads, traffic problems, high taxes, and a high cost of living. I was now looking forward to going to the Newark Field Office even more... This was going to be fun.

I joined a group of new agents arriving at the Newark Field Office where we were automatically relegated to moron status (said with affection but probably deserved on some levels). We were assigned to process applicant cases, conduct background check investigations, and address other basic organizational activities that were low in the office's hierarchy of program importance (actually at the bottom). We learned about the local Newark operating environment and were taught about basic paperwork protocols and local squad practices by several senior agents who worked in the office's applicant program. Basically, we were processing personnel packages for organizational hiring—not exactly the dangerous and daring special agent work that I was anticipating.

The senior agents in the applicant program were largely good folks who had grown tired later in their careers and wanted to work in FBI programs with less stress and more regular work schedules. A few of the senior agents were reportedly assigned to the applicant program to pay a penance for transgressions of some sort and were working their way out of administrative purgatory to get back to other more prestigious investigative programs. Overall, the senior agents in the Newark Field Office applicant program were helpful in providing us with a mostly kind and informative reception. They gave each of us a launching point to move toward an assignment with one of the office's operational squads. They disclosed the general "rules of the road," told us where some of the more obvious career potholes were and filled us in on important office dynamics and practices. They also told us about some basic field office customs and courtesies, so we knew how to behave ourselves. While this general course of instruction and orientation was good for new personnel, I would soon be provided with a few simple rules to live by that served me well throughout the rest of my FBI career.

Rules to Live By

One morning, a few of the senior agents (the "old breed," as I like to call them) gathered our group of new agents and took us to a conference room, closed the door, and began an informal but extremely useful orientation about how things "really worked" for FBI special agents. Before the discussion began, one of these senior agents told us that he was not admitting to being involved with, or guilty of, any activities that were outside of bureau policy. At this point, I was starting to wonder what I had gotten myself into, but this discussion was a blessing in disguise and gave me valuable insight on how to conduct business within my new organization. The senior agent's instructions on "how things work" consisted mainly of the following basic and non-negotiable (at least at that time) points of practice:

- **Do not mess with the government's money.** This carried a high likelihood of termination.
- **Do not misuse your bureau car.** This came with an automatic penalty of thirty days without pay.
- **Be careful with boyfriends and girlfriends in the office.** The social and professional consequences, if any, could be varied in nature but were risky on many levels.
- **Nobody but the special agent in charge of the field office speaks to the media. If you think you have something to say, think again—and then shut your mouth.** This valuable practice was once sacrosanct but was later eroded, along with other time-tested FBI norms, and became a cause of embarrassment, career damage, and even termination for some personnel. The eventual introduction of email, smartphones, chat tools, and social media created an environment

in which people could connect from afar and conduct business with varying levels of privacy and confidentiality; however, there was actually none of either on government systems. While these new communication capabilities were beneficial for expanded levels of collaboration that were previously unavailable, discipline quickly broke down—junior staff members could easily send email communications outside of their immediate chains of command without approval, thereby creating a new kind of workplace chaos. Some people became immortalized by their use of the "reply all" function, when funny or career-limiting content was shared with the entire organization. The FBI would later suffer instances of public embarrassment and unfavorable trial outcomes when unflattering or unprofessional email and chat traffic came to light in court proceedings and open-source media reports.

- **Above all else, <u>never embarrass the FBI</u>, no matter where you are, who you are with, or what you are doing.** This was the culture of the time—FBI personnel were always expected to dress properly, behave in a professional manner, show up on time, and be fully prepared to conduct the FBI director's business in an excellent fashion. Anything less was not acceptable for new agents and would be policed assertively by the old breed senior agents who believed that there was absolutely no excuse for a poor showing. Our reputation was built from our operational achievements, personal behavior, and displayed professionalism and would precede us everywhere we went and in everything we did. Our reputation would either enhance or detract from the image of the FBI, which was of the highest importance.

One of the senior agents closed out the discussion with a final thought: "You can win battles and lose the war across the course of your career." He advised us to be thoughtful about what we would complain about when we considered what we might be entitled to, what we felt the FBI owed us (in our minds—not theirs), or what the FBI should be doing for us. He concluded by telling us, "In the end, the FBI will owe us nothing, will expect everything, and will always get its pound of flesh." This bit of wisdom proved accurate as I learned through my own experiences, as well as those of my colleagues, in years to come.

Practical Lessons

The senior special agents who ran the Newark Field Office violent crime programs were considered the most capable and experienced manhunters we had. These agents were walking encyclopedias of knowledge that we could not get anywhere else. As a training and learning approach (as well as a way to get free labor), new agents would have the opportunity to go out with the "warrant squad" where FBI special agents and local law enforcement partners would work together apprehend dangerous criminals and fugitives in the Newark area. These were great training days when the FBI would enter the Prince Street housing projects (which have since been demolished) and seek out fugitives and other criminals for arrest. The Prince Street projects were known as one of the toughest and most dangerous areas in an already dangerous city. So, as new agents, on one of our first trips into the projects, we showed up with our belts jam-packed with guns, pepper spray, handcuffs, flashlights, impact weapons, protective gear, and other good stuff issued to us at the FBI Academy. Our senior agent counterparts showed up with their sidearms and one or two pairs of handcuffs. A few long guns may have been brought along as well, but that was about it.

We could not have looked more different coming from the same FBI field office. The senior agents explained that, through years of practical experience and guidance from their own mentors, they learned that agents seeking fugitives had to travel light because apprehensions could end up in foot chases and possible physical altercations. Having a heavy, weighed-down belt full of gear that looked like Batman's utility belt almost ensured that no successful arrests would be made if subjects decided to run. All told, we were weighed down with too much gear. This was contrary to what we were just recently taught at the FBI Academy, but it made sense (Lesson One).

On another occasion, one of the senior agents told us that we should always look up before entering the project buildings. The senior agents could see the confusion on our faces, so one of them explained, "People often know when we enter the projects. There have been times when people on the rooftops have pushed furniture off of roofs to distract law enforcement so they could flee." OK, looking up would now be a standard course of action (Lesson Two).

On a later trip with the warrant squad, as we approached a building, we were properly slimmed down on gear and made sure to look up and around before entering. It was a cold morning as we walked past a dead dog and took the stairs to reach the target apartment. (We were told to avoid elevators in the housing project buildings for fear of getting stuck.) We reached the target apartment and staged ourselves outside the door, with new agents to the rear. After someone answered the door, we went inside, and one of the senior agents whispered to us new agents that we should not lean on the walls, nor should we stay in one place too long without moving our feet. We were puzzled by these instructions, but we complied. It felt strange to be doing a continuous shuffle while trying to look like serious FBI agents.

We searched the apartment for a subject who appeared to have just been there. His belongings (keys, wallet, etc.) were on the nightstand, but we could not locate him. Everyone was confused about how he could have gotten out without us seeing him. While some of the senior agents talked with a few people in the apartment, somebody called out, saying that they found him. We moved to the sound of the callout. We were all stunned to see a naked man, who appeared to be about six and a half feet tall, standing in the kitchen. We wondered where he could have been as we searched the entire apartment. It turned out that this large man was able to wedge himself into a cabinet under the kitchen sink, which seemed too small for a man his size. He told us that he had practiced quickly getting himself into that space. We were taught that day to **never assume anything.** We **assumed** that someone could not be in a space just because of its size, so we did not look—we were mistaken (Lesson Three).

On the way out of the projects, one of the new agents asked about the instructions to not lean anywhere and to keep moving. The senior agent in charge said that the projects were full of roaches and other insects. If people leaned on the walls, roaches or other insects could get into hair or clothing. The continual movement and shuffling of feet made it more difficult for roaches and insects to crawl up pant legs (Lesson Four—I was sold on the value of experiential learning).

FILE REVIEW

The best way to gain valuable insight as a new member of a team or organization is to show up with your eyes, ears, and mind open and your mouth shut. The situational lessons presented in this chapter were not taught at the FBI Academy. They were the products of experience gained by people who have either learned from others or who have had to personally chase dangerous people, dodge falling furniture, conduct searches of the most ridiculous places, and evict insects from hair or clothing.

The last lesson is that you will always have a lot to learn from people who do a job and are good at it. Always be ready and willing to learn, do not depend on assumptions, and be willing to pass your knowledge and wisdom to others.

"Learn how to do hard things."

4

GETTING A TRAINING AGENT

I was fortunate in that, once I was assigned to the Newark Division's counterterrorism program, I was assigned a training agent (TA) who was to become a mentor in shaping my FBI values, beliefs, and practices. She was one of the more senior agents in the office's counterterrorism program and was a stickler for proper writing, documentation, and execution of case-related activities. My TA was fairly strict on how tasks were to be done (meaning properly with no shortcuts) and served as my primary instructor in everything ranging from routine investigative protocols/documentation to physical surveillance activities to technical surveillance operations. She was a former military officer and frequently highlighted the value of and requirement for proper operational case management. She was not receptive to shortcuts, indications of weak business management, or laziness (real or perceived). Under her tutelage, I eventually became a reasonably capable case agent (for a new guy), and I later began sharing some of her knowledge with some of my fellow new agents. As I look back on my career, I realize I was highly fortunate to have been mentored by my assigned TA. She started as my assigned trainer but ultimately became my mentor and then my friend.

I recall the morning that I met my TA. I was sitting at my temporary location in my new counterterrorism squad when a female agent poked her head into my room and asked my name. I replied and she said, "Good. I am your new training agent." She introduced herself (hereafter referred to as Amelia) and then told me to grab my things. This would be my first trip to some of the target operating areas for "area familiarization."

While she drove, I sat and listened as she pointed out key streets and locations. While we were moving through the city, I noticed that there were no street signs. Amelia looked at me and said, "Buy some maps. The people here continually steal the street signs, and the city has stopped putting them back up." As we were driving through some of the rougher areas, Amelia said, "Look. When you are in this part of town and when it is safe to do so, do not stop completely at stop signs. Look around, make sure it is safe, and roll through." I was not sure why she suggested this. She must have seen my confusion, so she sighed and said, "If you stop in these areas, there is a good chance you could get carjacked. You will then have to decide if you are going to shoot someone to get away and save yourself and your bureau vehicle." I thought she was joking at first, but she was not—at least I did not think she was. She then smiled and we drove along.

This car ride defined our relationship, which I value to this day. After this area-familiarization ride, we would take many rides together where she provided advice and instruction on being an FBI agent, told me how to follow procedures, and gave me various "old breed" perspectives to consider as I later navigated the operating environment alone to meet informants, conduct physical surveillance, and avoid getting carjacked.

New Agent Education

From my time in military service, I recognized the value of properly training people and helping them to do their jobs, as I had been both a military trainee and a trainer. That said, my experience as a new agent further refined my views on the necessity of good training provided by high-quality, conscientious mentors who were also competent leaders. While I had a great TA in Amelia, I remember that some of my fellow new agents struggled to adapt to the demands of the FBI because they were not provided with what I felt were enthusiastic (or conscientious) trainers and mentors. These less-than-enthusiastic mentors failed to teach the cardinal points of the FBI's organizational and investigative culture, which, at the most basic level, was to be current, accurate, and thorough in everything. Some of my fellow new agents ran into case management challenges because they learned procedural shortcuts first and then used shortcuts on shortcuts in some of their investigative approaches. Unfortunately, some of my new agent colleagues developed poor attitudes and questionable work practices based on what they were taught, observed, or missed out on.

One day, while a TA was training an assigned new agent, one of the more capable and respected senior agents on the squad pulled me aside and said, "See that guy (the training agent)? He has almost twenty years of experience. The problem is that he has twenty times of one year's worth of experience. Learn how to do hard things. Do not be that guy." After that short conversation, I began to look for areas of weakness in my own performance and sought out solutions for my own shortfalls such as lack of depth or understanding; surface-level knowledge; drifting toward doing easier things; and allowing myself to fall into less-than-enthusiastic approaches. I could always count on Amelia to give me a wake-up call and get me back in line with her standards, for which I was thankful.

In hindsight, I was just plain lucky to have Amelia as my assigned TA, and I helped as many of my teammates as I could with certain basic procedures and processes, but being a new agent myself, I was limited in what I could offer. I do not know how all of my Newark new agent colleagues fared throughout their careers, but some of them were not getting a good start. I did not know it at the time, but my eyes were being opened to organizational erosion on a local scale. The same erosion that was likely happening in other offices. Later in my career, I saw some of the larger, more strategic effects of this erosion, which were probably contributing factors to shortfalls in general FBI leadership, competence, and professionalism.

Task Force Guidance

Another source of training and wisdom for new agents came from the task force members I was fortunate to serve with. The FBI counterterrorism operating model at the time (mid-1990s) was relatively new and was known as the Joint Terrorism Task Force or simply JTTF. Under the JTTF model, select members of various federal, state, and local law enforcement communities (and sometimes intelligence community and Department of Defense components) were provided with special federal deputation and top-secret security clearances. These task force members would then work alongside FBI special agents to investigate classified national security matters such as terrorism and weapons of mass destruction programs. Many of these task force officers, or TFOs, were veteran members in their agencies. They served as a wealth of information, perspective, training, essential contacts, and general law enforcement cultural guidelines for new FBI agents. As we gained their trust and support, these TFOs taught us how operations worked (or should have worked) outside of the FBI ecosystem. They introduced us to people who would make us more effective in gaining access to essential information that helped to make a successful investigation.

Getting a Training Agent

From these TFOs, I learned about the sometimes-complex dynamics between federal, state, and local law enforcement organizations and how to navigate some of the cultural divides and historical friction points among law enforcement partners. I learned how to develop strong relationships with the TFOs and liaison contacts, as well as their organizations. I learned quickly how to treat people with professional respect and found that partnerships were vital to any sustained successful investigative or operational effort. I was glad to receive the tutelage and guidance of these experienced law enforcement professionals. They had their own organizational cultures that they were willing to subordinate to some degree to fit into the FBI JTTF working environment. I knew I had to live up to the expectations they had for the FBI and its investigative staff members.

In one instance, another agent and I were reporting to the Newark International Airport (now Liberty Airport) to address a bomb threat matter. I was fortunate that one of our senior JTTF TFOs was also moving toward the airport and would meet us there. Once my partner agent and I arrived, the TFO pointed to an area that was clearly marked NO PARKING and told us to park there. I was uncomfortable doing so, but I reluctantly followed his instructions. When we exited our car, we walked up to the TFO, who was talking with a few Port Authority Police Department officers. The TFO introduced us as being with the FBI in Newark and as working with the TFO on the Joint Terrorism Task Force. The other agent presented his federal credentials to identify himself, and then I did the same. The Port Authority police officers looked at us with a bit of disdain and continued their conversation with the TFO. We were given some baseline information from the police officers, and we agreed to meet up back in the TFO's office to compare notes in our field office squad area.

After we compared notes, my FBI partner departed the TFO's office. I was about to leave the room when the TFO asked me to stay. He said he wanted to share some advice with me, so I would have an easier time during my next visit to Newark Airport. I told him that I would appreciate his feedback.

He advised me that, when introduced to police officers by another police officer, I should not show my federal credentials unless someone asked. To do so without being asked was considered pompous and unnecessary and would make the officers think I was a self-important jerk. This was enlightening, as I was just following the lead of my partner. I told him this, and the TFO nodded and said that the other FBI agent was not very highly regarded at the airport. Then he told me that I would get further with the Port Authority officers by being a courteous, humble federal agent and seeking their input and suggestions before doing anything.

The TFO also knew that I was uncomfortable parking where he directed, which, to my ignorance, was actually an area designated for visiting law enforcement or emergency vehicles. He said that my reluctance to park there showed inexperience, a lack of confidence, and an absence of command presence. He advised that, if I was ever challenged for parking there, I should inform Port Authority officers that I was with the FBI and then ask for the officer's help in finding the people handling the bomb threat or other pertinent issue. I had no idea about this protocol, and I thanked him for letting me know.

I then asked if my partner agent knew about these things. The TFO said he did not know and did not care, as he felt that my partner agent would not listen anyway. After this discussion, I used the TFO's general approach for the rest of my career when dealing with most everyone and found great success in interpersonal interactions at all levels.

That TFO taught me that humility, courtesy, and an earnest request for assistance will almost always garner a favorable response. Through his example and that of others, I learned to treat everyone with respect and dignity. No one cares for pomposity or flaring egos—especially when someone does not know what they are doing.

Ownership and Outcomes

I learned to focus on taking ownership in my work and obtaining expected outcomes. My TA and TFO mentors stressed a high degree of ownership of my cases, files, paperwork, human intelligence sources, relationships, successes, and failures. That said, I did not find a pervasive culture of such ownership across the FBI at later points in my career. I began to see that the people who were trusted, respected, and revered carried high levels of ownership. Conversely, others who held little to no respect did not carry ownership, so they were not trusted and were sometimes treated with open disdain.

I made a lot of mistakes as a new agent (and throughout my career), but I did my best to assume all of the blame for poor outcomes. I made it a practice to quickly seek guidance or assistance in resolving shortfalls, and to put in measures that would preclude future similar shortfalls. The senior agents and TFOs understood that new agents would make mistakes, and they were willing to assist and support our efforts. But their support was limited once people began casting blame on others, making excuses, or seeking to relieve themselves of culpability for negative outcomes.

I became a firm believer in the old saying, "The buck stops here." I learned a great lesson in ownership from watching

FBI Director Freeh as he testified before a congressional committee about the FBI's counterintelligence investigation into the activities of Wen Ho Lee. Lee was of Chinese heritage and worked at the Los Alamos National Laboratory when he was accused of spying for China and stealing secrets associated with the US nuclear program. According to various accounts, this investigation may not have been conducted as well as it could have been by the FBI, and Lee was eventually freed on a plea deal.

What is germane to this conversation is that, during congressional testimony, Director Freeh was queried about the FBI's counterintelligence investigation for Lee. After several statements regarding questionable FBI case management and less-than-expected investigative results, Director Freeh was asked about potential failures and lack of performance on the part of the assigned FBI investigators. Instead of allowing this discussion to develop further, Director Freeh exhibited something not frequently seen in the more recent era of FBI senior leadership: ownership. He stopped the line of questioning and advised the congressional committee members that as the FBI director, accountability for any real or perceived shortfalls stopped with him. He declared that there would be no criticism of his people. I was floored and I thought that Director Freeh's display of ownership for what was seen as an unsuccessful case was impressive. It set a standard for the rest of my FBI career—especially when I was fortunate to move into various leadership roles. I frequently recalled that exchange between Director Freeh and the congressional committee and often used it as the standard for protecting my staff members from unearned criticism when they worked with maximum personal effort, within established operating parameters, and within leadership intent but still met with shortfalls in expected outcomes.

Over the next several years, I received a highly accelerated education (both formal and informal) on various counterterrorism operational methodologies, legal authorities, technical collection, law enforcement etiquette, case management, human intelligence operations, administrative procedures, and general personal and professional development. These skills were necessary for successfully conducting operations, managing investigative activities, building relationships, and leading work teams. My TA, Amelia, eventually moved on to another assignment, so my squad colleagues and I built upon her success and even created some new approaches. We worked closely as we built a successful operational program around the investigation of publicly known Palestinian rejectionist groups such as Hamas, the Palestinian Islamic Jihad, the Popular Front for the Liberation of Palestine, and their associated support networks. We did some strong work with international and domestic security partners in interdicting terrorist support and logistics networks and possibly inhibiting military wing operations for these groups. We thought we were doing well and that we had our threat environment well characterized. We became complacent (again), and I was proven wrong in September 2001.

An unidentified group of people was operating in our area that would play a significant part in the events of September 11, 2001. We did not know it then, but the terrorist hijacking team that would take control of United Flight 93 was covertly operating in our geographic area. Important lessons on international terrorism, ownership, and leadership were waiting for me in September 2001.

FILE REVIEW

I learned to treat all of my assignments with beneficial ownership. I treated responsibilities and expectations entrusted to me as if they were my own—even when they were not. I took full ownership of everything associated with the potential success and mission accomplishment of my assigned tasks, projects, programs, tactical goals, and strategic objectives.

When I was privileged to lead people and programs, I followed Director Freeh's example by owning all shortfalls and ensuring that my staff owned all successes and achievements. I also learned to identify and discourage the development of malignant ownership that ultimately led to ego problems, turf battles, and self-interested decision-making that held the organization back or damaged the organization's ability to achieve its mission or purpose.

I used these approaches to take beneficial ownership and to protect my leaders, colleagues, and staff members when they did their best to meet mission needs but still failed or encountered shortfalls. Such failures or shortfalls are sometimes the cost of doing business and should be treated accordingly whenever possible. To paraphrase Lt. General Hal Moore (USA, Retired) in looking at shortfalls or failures, he said three strikes and you are not out… there is always something else you can do.

" The FBI would soon find itself enveloped in a hurricane of doubt, blame, and change that would dominate its existence."

5

A DEFINING MOMENT FOR THE FBI, THE UNITED STATES, AND THE WORLD

September 11, 2001, was a watershed day for everyone around the world. Many reports, books, and accounts have been written about the events and outcomes of that day. For this book, I will provide some of my personal experience on a general level. In this forum, I cannot do justice to the evil, grief, loss, and heroism that characterized the events on September 11, 2001, or other related events that followed.

The Day That Changed Everything

That fateful day started in a fairly routine manner for the FBI's Newark Field Office with lots of sunshine and heavy daily traffic on all roadways that led to New York City. My squad supervisor was scheduled to arrive at the office a bit later that morning. As my counterterrorism squad's principal relief supervisor (the nominal second in charge), I went to the squad supervisor's office to process mail, check email, find out what had to be done for the day, and get things ready for my supervisor's arrival.

As the morning wore on, everything was proceeding normally until one of the squad's intelligence research specialists moved quickly through the hallways announcing that an aircraft had struck one of the World Trade Center towers. I looked out the office window and, across the river, I could see smoke rising from the first tower strike. I thought, "Damn, that is going to make for a really bad day for some folks. I hope not many people were injured." Everyone within earshot in the squad area initially thought that a small commuter aircraft accidentally struck one of the towers, but we had a lot more coming at us, fast and hard.

We would quickly find ourselves stunned and operating in a VUCA-dominated environment that day and for years to come. VUCA is an acronym attributed to the US Army's analysis of the global threat environment that took form in the early 1990s, after the fall of the Soviet Union. The world went from a relatively stable model of two super-power countries existing in perceived parity to an environment that was suddenly characterized by **V**olatility, **U**ncertainty, **C**onfusion, and **A**mbiguity. This environment was caused by a political vacuum and the resultant reshuffling of world power, political maneuvering, and societal dominance that would follow. The FBI would soon find itself in a full VUCA environment and we would be completely overwhelmed before we knew it.

For additional context, we should step back and look at the communications and information management environment that was in place for the FBI circa 2001. Contrary to what some people might believe, the FBI was not a highly technology-driven organization at that time.

Leading up to 2001, the bureau did not even have widespread deployment of televisions and cable communications services throughout its offices to support situational awareness. There was no broad use of cellular telephones by field personnel. Internet-based communications and services had not yet graduated from dial-up modems and had not yet come into their own. There was no Wi-Fi for common use. There were no cellular or internet data resources (no Google, X, Google Maps, Facebook, WhatsApp, etc.) that many people have had at their disposal for nearly their entire lives.

As a point of reference, just before September 11, 2001, the FBI Newark Division had finally received an office-wide public branch exchange voice mail system. Prior to the arrival of this system, Newark agents had to purchase their own cassette tape answering machines to catch missed telephone calls at their desks. Teletypes and fax machines were still being used as primary means of moving priority expedited communications.

For other more routine FBI communications, we used interoffice paper-based mail systems and third-party paid service providers that physically moved mail throughout the FBI's infrastructure. My counterterrorism squad was considered fortunate in that we had just received pagers with onboard text messaging capability, which was considered "high tech" at the time. The main problem was that we could only communicate by text with each other because most agents in other programs still had older pagers that operated on numerical communications data only.

The analyst who made the initial notifications on the first World Trade Center strike was listening to an FM radio in his office when he heard about and then announced the second tower strike. At that point, we all knew that something bad was happening, but we were somewhat paralyzed by a lack of information, poor situational awareness, and an absence of operational models to work from in developing initial plans of action.

We were trying to make telephone calls to find out what was going on; however, much of the commercial communications in the immediate New York City metropolitan area suffered massive degradation after the destruction of the World Trade Center towers. The subsequent flood of communications traffic quickly overwhelmed and paralyzed remaining systems. Most of the communication systems at that time generally did not communicate with each other and offered no planned redundancy for emergency situations.

What many people did not realize was that the World Trade Center was home to a number of antenna arrays that stopped transmitting when the towers fell. Functional communications were terribly interrupted. At the time, there were no dedicated communication networks for law enforcement, fire departments, emergency services, and other public safety/emergency management organizations established for integrated and coordinated operations.

To make matters worse, the FBI New York Field Office, which was the bureau's largest and arguably most capable field component, was largely taken out of short-term operation by the destruction and chaos that ensued. The FBI, as a whole, found itself operationally blinded, working from fragmentary incident information, managing multiple terror attack sites, trying to account for its personnel in affected terror sites, and struggling to muster a proper initial crisis response to the worst terror attack ever committed against the United States and its people on our native soil.

We had a long day and night ahead of us as we tried to figure out what was going on. We were also trying to secure a common operating perspective between FBI headquarters and all other field offices to determine if any other terror attacks were planned that had not yet been executed. People were scared, angry, confused, and generally shocked at the enormity of what happened that day. The FBI was not ready for that kind of catastrophe, and neither were other US government agencies nor the public.

The Pre-9/11 Operating Environment

Prior to September 2001, the Counterterrorism Program was a much lower priority for the FBI. The approach for many of the smaller field offices was a checkbox process to cover assigned investigative leads from other offices, make a few rudimentary database checks, hit minimum investigative steps to cover administrative compliance requirements, and file the necessary paperwork for case file reviews and inspection audits. FBI case agents were expected to complete a series of database checks and various basic investigative actions within a set timeframe. These case agents would be expected to positively identify a subject and determine if the information gathered would support established investigative requirements for an extended investigation or justify more advanced investigative activities.

Circa September 2001, the preliminary inquiry was the starting point in the counterterrorism investigative cycle when a case agent would indicate the identification of a subject and the basis of the investigation. If approved by a supervisor, the agent would conduct required investigative activities and research to determine if further scrutiny or more in-depth, higher-level investigative work would be required.

If more work was required, the case agent would then submit a request to FBIHQ to initiate a full field investigation. This action, if approved, provided case funding and the authority to conduct more sophisticated activities such as undercover operations, technical surveillance, and other sensitive intelligence collection measures to further identify and mitigate possible threats and interdict terror-related activities.

Some of the larger FBI field offices, such as New York, Los Angeles, and Chicago, had sophisticated, more capable counterterrorism programs. But most of the mid- to small-sized field offices had fairly rudimentary programs. These smaller offices lacked the necessary training, skills, focus, and operational leadership to seek out and engage terrorists, their associates, and related support networks. Many field offices did not have the training or resources to conduct sensitive investigative and intelligence activities to detect, deter, and defeat Al Qaeda terror operations before they could harm people or damage property. None of these shortfalls were the fault of any one person or group, but it was just the way things were at that time.

While we thought the FBI was doing a reasonably good job in the counterterrorism realm, I learned firsthand that we, in fact, suffered from a lack of imagination, an inadequate sense of investigative curiosity, and an absence of a sense of urgency. These factors and others converged to provide a permissive operating environment that our Al Qaeda adversaries were able to successfully exploit. After all of the excuses and reasons for why some things happened and others did not, the bottom line was that we had our asses kicked.

Examination of Insufficient Efforts

I spoke with one of our valued international liaison partners shortly before September 11, 2001, and found out that we did not know nearly enough about our adversaries from certain cultural and operational perspectives. This liaison partner saw the FBI's bureaucratic and administrative approaches to counterterrorism as being wholly insufficient (and somewhat laughable to them) in dealing with an evolving threat environment and an emerging adversary that was ultimately capable of planning and executing missions that the FBI would be unable to detect and counter.

When I look back, I do not assign blame to anyone. This was an organizational shortfall that no one person on any level could have prevented. The FBI, as an institution, lacked the

operational vision, organizational leadership, and warrior spirit that were needed to proactively identify and directly engage the Al-Qaeda threat.

The FBI, as a whole, was not proactive, predictive, or protective in its operations. We did not create a hostile operating environment for the terrorists. We did not engage terrorists assertively, domestically or abroad, and force them to change their behaviors. We did not pressure them into abandoning hardened targets or high consequence environments. Aside from some of the larger, more capable field offices previously mentioned, the FBI was going through the motions, in most instances, to meet administrative requirements. As a result, the FBI would soon find itself enveloped in a hurricane of doubt, blame, and change that would dominate its existence over the next decade.

September 11, 2001, and its aftermath were world-changing, and the worldwide consequences clearly warrant a separate, dedicated discussion, of which there have already been many. The scope of this discussion could not do proper justice to the immediate and consequential repercussions on all the victims, families, and persons impacted by the events surrounding the World Trade Center; the Pentagon; the Shanksville, Pennsylvania site; the FBI; the United States; and the rest of the world.

FILE REVIEW

Whatever your resource base might be, it will be quickly overwhelmed and overextended in handling crisis management operations, investigations, security, communications, intelligence, information management, transportation, damage control, medical/first aid, and connecting with partner organizations. Trusting technology to work during a crisis is a sure way to fail unless proper training and function testing are regularly conducted in the course of regular business.

Not having proven standard operating procedures or viable emergency plans will create paralysis and fear, which impede an effective operational response. But having these procedures will not help if people are not familiar with them, are not trained in their execution, and are unable to muster for assigned emergency duties. Proper training, prioritization, and exercises are crucial steps toward mounting a relevant response to a crisis event. Strong, capable leadership will be the key to success during any crisis or emergency—there is no substitute.

"I continued to learn about managing squad operations and leading others while I worked through the challenges associated with September 11th and the rising effects of uncertainty and acute fatigue on the FBI and its people."

6

GOING TO FBI HEADQUARTERS

Shortly after September 11, 2001, my squad supervisor, who was a memorable and exemplary leader and mentor, departed the Newark office for a previously awarded promotion to FBI Headquarters (FBIHQ) in Washington, DC.

This supervisor would be sorely missed by our squad as well as other field office personnel as he was a highly competent, respected, and well-liked senior agent. He treated everyone fairly, kindly, and respectfully. I learned many things from watching him interact with people while I worked under his leadership. He also showed me how to perform the operational and administrative activities that were necessary to sustain squad-level business. He let me participate directly in preparations for field office inspections, and he showed me how to conduct proper file reviews. Through all of these activities, he helped me to be successful in the Newark office. His mentorship and support in the early part of my career led to many of my future successes. I would miss him as a professional mentor and friend. He will always be "El Jefe".

Moving Forward

As the second in charge of the squad at that time, I became the acting squad supervisor until I was scheduled to depart in February 2002 for a promotion to serve as a supervisory special agent in the FBIHQ counterterrorism program. I was fortunate to have the opportunity to directly oversee squad operations for a while and I kept the squad moving forward as best as I knew how, with a lot of help and patience from my colleagues.

I continued to learn about managing squad operations and leading others while I worked through the challenges associated with September 11th—related crisis management, consequence management, and the rising effects of uncertainty and acute fatigue on the FBI and its people. I watched coworkers in the Newark Field Office grieve in their own ways, and I also saw a sense of organizational uncertainty begin to set in. This uncertainty was prevalent in the field office's previously top-tier criminal investigative programs, which appeared to take a long-term back seat to the terrorism investigative storm that had consumed the FBI. Generally, against their wishes, the bureau's vaunted criminal investigative programs were moved into the daily processing of counterterrorism investigative leads and supporting the FBI's new PENTTBOMB major case, which covered all of the terrorist case activities associated with September 11th.

Forming Leadership Practices

Looking back, I realize that the special agents of Newark criminal investigative programs were not properly informed on what was happening, why program priorities were shifting, or what their short-term roles would be in supporting post-September 11th operations. The agents were not given the "why" of what was going on as matter of professional courtesy and leadership engagement. The criminal program agents were professionals and were willing to help, but they soon became resentful and unhappy due to what appeared to be a general lack of leadership, no information, and a lack of consideration for their respective investigative programs and duties.

Basically, many of these agents felt that no one cared enough to talk with them. Before my squad supervisor departed the division, I gained a small but important insight into forming leadership practices that helped me care for personnel during a crisis (and most other times).

In one instance, my supervisor and I attended an off-site meeting and were returning to our office building in downtown Newark. At the parking garage entry gate, armed FBI special agents were checking identification. After the events of September 11, the field office's senior leaders thought it would be prudent to increase physical security around the building, hence the overt presence of the armed agents.

When we moved our car up to the gate, my supervisor rolled down the window and talked with the sentries. Instead of simply flashing his credentials and driving through the gate with windows up as other people tended to do, he stopped and talked with the gate crew for less than a minute.

He asked them how they were doing and if they needed anything. He also asked if they needed a break to get something to eat or to use the restroom. While no one took him up on his offer, the appreciation that I saw on those agents' faces was incredible—someone in a field office leadership role actually cared enough to stop and sincerely ask about their welfare.

This was a valuable lesson. I knew from that point forward that part of my responsibility was to look out for the general welfare of people—not just my own crew, but everyone who needed help or could be helped, crisis or no crisis.

On another day, as I returned to the office building from off-site activities, I noticed that one person filled the gate sentry duty: a division senior agent who served as a polygraph examiner. This polygrapher role was generally treated with more respect and deference than common case agents;

however, times were different now, and no one was exempt from routine physical security or sentry duty.

I pulled up to the gate, rolled down my window, and said hello. I then asked if he needed anything. I offered to send someone down to relieve him for a bit, which he declined with thanks. I then asked if I could send down some coffee or anything else. He said no, but then he looked at me and said that I was the only person, all day, to ask him how he was doing or if he needed anything. He said thank you and that he was OK. It seemed to mean a lot to him.

The takeaway here is that this person, who had previously been given deferential treatment because of his polygrapher role, was now standing on gate sentry duty and was not happy. The fact that someone stopped to check on him seemed to make a difference in his day. His entire demeanor changed during our short conversation.

I hoped that he felt, even for a moment, that someone cared. From then on, I always tried to provide some sort of recognition of the situations of others and to offer assistance or support whenever I could. It made a lot of difference throughout my FBI leadership career when managing crises or stressful times, and I hope that I was able to make people's days a bit better whenever I could. I learned that even a small sincere gesture of interest in people's welfare and well-being can be restorative to personnel morale and willingness to endure hardship for the mission.

My time in Newark taught me that, as a colleague and leader in crisis environments, it is essential to treat others with professional candor, kindness, and as much transparency as possible to ensure that they know what is happening and why, what is expected of them, and how they fit into the current operational environment. As a leader, I learned that even the smallest sincere interest in people's welfare and wellbeing can boost morale and their willingness to endure unfavorable circumstances.

One last lesson I learned in managing crises was the importance of maintaining a sense of humor. This includes letting some things slide and not taking offense to certain actions or words spoken in fear, fatigue, or anxiety. (Not that many things would be considered funny during a crisis, but there may be time for fond recall of certain instances later.) This perspective could (and did) go a long way for me in preserving relationships and reducing friction during high stress situations.

A New Assignment

I took my post-September 11th experiences with me as I began transitioning to leave the known in the Newark office to go to the unknown at FBIHQ. While the aftermath of the events of September 11th continued with sustained fury, I reported for FBIHQ duty in February 2002 to serve as a newly minted supervisory special agent in the FBI's now highly prioritized, scrutinized, and brutalized counterterrorism program.

I was again a low-level grunt. I was effectively relegated to new agent status in the FBIHQ hierarchy, even though I was now a supervisory special agent. I was joining an injured and insulted FBI counterterrorism program that was still underfunded, understaffed, and in some ways, still under-prioritized in the face of the enormous impact of September 11th. Little did I know that this assignment was the beginning of an operational, professional, and personal marathon that would be physically and psychologically taxing in ways that I had not yet experienced or envisioned.

This is where I met the two FBIHQ intelligence operations specialists (IOSs) who would supposedly be working for me in managing a host of terror-related threat matters in the Radical Fundamentalist Unit. These IOSs, Bonnie and Clyde, were intelligence professionals, not special agents. Yet they were my superiors in most every way that I could see. They knew more than I did about most everything. They were substantive program management experts for various threat issues and terrorist groups—some of which I had never heard of. They were smarter than I was and were highly experienced in how to process Foreign Intelligence Surveillance Act (FISA) electronic surveillance authorization packages for submission from FBIHQ to the Department of Justice to the Foreign Intelligence Surveillance Court (FISC).

Bonnie and Clyde were outstanding, and even though I was nominally in charge of them, I worked for them. The only task they could not do that I could was to serve as an affiant and swear out surveillance affidavits before the FISC. That said, they were kind and receptive, and they helped me to learn the arcane ways of FBIHQ. They skillfully taught me the ins and outs of FISA administrative matters and FISC applications and affidavits while they patiently schooled me on various threat issues and terrorist groups.

Over time, we became a good team. I valued them highly as they gave me a fighting chance to survive in the post-September 11th FBIHQ world. They helped me to see a broader view of operations and we worked together to manage difficult discussions with FBI field offices that were struggling to operate in the bureau's new counterterrorism context. These experiences would help to forge my future views and practices.

FILE REVIEW

Leadership and learning go hand in hand. I was supposed to be in charge in my new FBIHQ role, but I was the least capable and least knowledgeable member of my small team with Bonnie and Clyde. I am glad I showed up with my eyes, ears, and mind open and my mouth shut. I listened, learned, and built good relationships with my teammates.

There was never any discussion about my being in charge or about Bonnie and Clyde working for me. We knew our roles, and I treated them with respect and courtesy. I also deferred to them or gave them input in operational matters whenever I could.

I found that being in charge did not mean that I was the smartest or best at anything. As a leader, I held a different set of responsibilities. It was my job to take care of Bonnie and Clyde while I made sure they had the required top cover, resourcing, and backing to run challenging operations. I sheltered them from hostile calls from field offices and protected them as much as I could from the chronic bullshit that was pervasive at FBIHQ at the time.

I still recall those days, and I thank Bonnie and Clyde for helping me to understand the why, what, and how of counterterrorism operations management. I took the leadership and program management lessons they shared and used them throughout the rest of my career.

Final thought: There is no reason to tell people that you are in charge. If you have to tell people who are better at everything than you are that you are in charge, then you are not in charge.

"The FBI had to brace itself, refocus, and embrace a new sense of warriorship to survive and possibly thrive again."

7

COUNTERTERRORISM DIVISION AND A TRANSITIONING FBIHQ

In the post-September 11th world, the FBI was overextended, overtaxed, overwhelmed, and overmatched, and it was conducting business in survival mode every day. The constant criticism from congressional leaders and the shaken faith of the American public weighed heavily on the bureau and its senior organizational leaders. The duty hours were long, and the prevailing counterterrorism operations environment was harsh and unforgiving while we sought to bring all those associated with the September 11th attacks to justice. We were also working ourselves to death as we were concurrently working to identify and interdict any further terror attacks against the US and its people.

The FBIHQ intermediate leadership cadre (think mid-level management) was under immense pressure every day. On the working level, I watched my fellow counterterrorism agents and analysts go through various levels of fear, anxiety, frustration, and physical exhaustion. Some people actually experienced physical or emotional breakdowns over time. I regularly saw people crying at their desks, and many were having health issues and family problems.

In 2003, an experienced counterterrorism supervisory special agent killed himself with his own service weapon after reportedly receiving an early morning call from FBIHQ. (These regular early morning HQ calls were dreaded by all counterterrorism managers.) It was never made clear if there was a correlation between this tragic event and the punishing FBIHQ work environment, but I will offer the situation to characterize the intensity of what was going on at the time.

After this tragedy, FBIHQ senior leadership knew that something had to change to manage the organization's updated counterterrorism mission and to sustain effective operations. The previous FBI counterterrorism operating models adopted circa 1999 were no longer adequate, so the Counterterrorism Division (CTD) was reorganized with an updated program management structure in early 2003.

The Impact of an Effective FBI Leader

As we, the standing CTD workforce, migrated into our new organizational structure and program management roles, I met my new unit chief (hereafter referred to as "Patton") for the first time. Patton was a warrior, a leader, and a true believer (at the time) in the FBI and its mission. He was a former police officer, and he exemplified mission dedication to an almost maniacal level. He showed all of us the importance of ensuring sharp execution, keeping track of assignments, meeting timelines and deadlines, and performing supervisory follow-up to ensure that operational needs were met, and standards were maintained.

Patton was an imposing taskmaster, and he kept a notebook everywhere he went. He always wrote everything down (all of the time), and he used his notes to remember what was supposed to be done and when (all of the time). With Patton's direct counsel (to be explained later), I adopted this same practice, and it served me well for the remainder of my career. I liked Patton, even with his intense business approach,

Counterterrorism Division and a Transitioning FBIHQ

because I generally knew where I stood with him, and he would back me up when I ran into conflict with more senior FBIHQ managers or field office senior managers. However, some people did not like working for Patton because they felt he was too tough. Without a doubt, he was tough. He was tough on people whom he believed were lazy or whom he identified as dodging responsibility or not pulling their weight. He was tough on people who gave minimal effort to get by or people who did not follow through to meet deadlines and objectives. Patton was definitely tough, but that was what the FBI needed at the time.

Patton exemplified the warriorship that the circumstances surrounding September 11th called for from the FBI. Unfortunately, his kind of warriorship was inconsistent, at best, or missing completely among other FBIHQ mid-level managers. As time wore on after September 11, 2001, the FBI started becoming more risk-averse, and operations were being governed by people who were eager to avoid problems. Aside from Patton and a few others I encountered, many FBI managers became fearful of reprisal for any actual or perceived shortfalls, and some managers flat out refused to extend themselves and take calculated risks. When we needed bravery and assertiveness from our leaders to get our confidence back and to show the way forward, we instead received ass-covering and waffling that only served to further erode morale.

Patton helped me (and sometimes forced me) to see that the FBI had to brace itself, refocus, and embrace a new sense of warriorship to survive and possibly thrive again. I found that I had to step up and improve myself to meet the standards and expectations set by Patton. While it was not enjoyable at the time, the experience made me a better agent and a stronger person.

Leadership Preparation

As noted earlier, the bureau had just had its ass kicked by a determined adversary. In Patton's mind, it was not the time to tend to our wounds and feel sorry for ourselves, but it was time to increase performance and intensity in terms of mission focus, execution, and follow up. Also, Patton had no qualms about giving out a public reprimand when warranted, which became an unsatisfactory practice when the FBI began moving toward a new era of modern management principles in its leadership channels. As previously highlighted, Patton provided me with a lesson that changed my view on the practice of carrying a notebook and being prepared to take meeting notes for proper operational recall, tracking, and follow up. It was a somewhat silly instance, but it shaped my thoughts in many subsequent areas and activities.

One day, Patton called an impromptu meeting for our entire unit to discuss an operational development and asked everyone to come to his office immediately. I got up from my desk and walked to his office, and with my fellow program managers, I sat and listened to the brief. At one point, Patton looked at me, and in his own charming way, he asked why I was not taking notes and why did I not bring anything to write on. He also asked how I would remember the details he was providing. He gave me a disgusted look and went on with his brief.

After the meeting ended, I was mad and embarrassed (which, in retrospect, was immature of me). Sure, I was mad at Patton for the public reprimand, but as I thought about it, I became more mad at myself—not him. He was right. I was not prepared for a meeting with my supervisor. I failed to take a few seconds to grab a pen and paper. Was this a lack of focus or respect on my part? Did I give the impression that what Patton was saying was not important to me? Would I actually recall everything he talked about so I could take appropriate follow-up actions?

All of these thoughts rattled around in my mind. In hindsight, I appreciated Patton's public counseling. For the rest of my career, I never showed up to any future meeting without pen and paper. I actually made it a priority to plan and prepare for meetings and discussions with my supervisors. When I began holding my own meetings, I always encouraged people to bring those items so they could capture details, tasks, deadlines, or other information essential for mission success. I appreciated Patton's instruction, and I made sure to never again leave myself unprepared, as a leader or as a staff member.

My views changed and improved in showing proper respect and interest as I interacted with my leaders, colleagues, and staff members. Always having pen and paper with me became part of my professional responsibilities, no matter who I was meeting with or what I was doing. I saw the importance of taking notes and not relying solely on my memory, whether we had simple or complicated operational tasks to accomplish—it did not matter which. I began consistently logging timelines and deadlines so I could measure my effort, determine resource needs and allocations, and provide a finished product or service within allotted processing cycles. I also adopted the philosophy that no good special agent should ever be without pen and paper (similar to the practice of good engineers). It was all about being prepared and ready to act. As Patton and I later parted ways (when we both received promotions), I look back on my time with him fondly and with appreciation for the example he set for my CTD ITOS 1 colleagues and me.

A Transitioning FBI

Post-September 11th life in CTD remained hard on all fronts, so the FBIHQ senior leadership apparently believed that making the program atmosphere less demanding would attract more workers to fill crucial, unfilled positions. At the time, CTD was chronically understaffed due to the harsh working conditions that were well known across the bureau. As a good-morning greeting in CTD, we received a kick to the shins to get the day started. As thanks for a hard CTD day's work, we received a kick in the ass on our way out. At the same time, FBIHQ senior leaders were receiving heavy pressure from congressional leaders to fill funded, vacant positions as quickly as possible. Life at FBIHQ remained hard, harsh, and demanding. It was an environment that either forged leaders or broke people. Somehow, in this environment, the FBI began its march toward more "modern" leadership models and practices.

Looking back on the FBI's transition to updated, more modern leadership models (meaning softer, kinder, and more in touch with people's feelings), I believe that the bureau would have done much better in the long run if it had promoted more leaders like Patton, who taught us how to be tough, resilient, unflappable, competent, and accountable. His leadership and operating models would have been more beneficial in strategically building strong future leaders versus the sometimes weak and ineffective, yet more popular, "servant leader" folks who later showed up to the CTD meat grinder and across other FBIHQ programs.

Filling positions with supposedly more likable, easy-going leaders might have been a popular approach in the short term, but these kinds of leaders often struggled to withstand the demands of the highly intense and corrosive CTD operations environment. These leaders often created more staff problems, fatigue, and burnout in an already challenging leadership environment. These same types of leaders would later advance into senior FBI leadership positions and bring their "likable" ways with them, thereby planting the seeds for future organizational erosion and mediocrity.

I believe that the general softening of the FBI's leadership approaches and requirements through the early to mid-2000s led to the adoption of a less effective program management environment. This development became poisonous and led to significant cultural changes and bad stop-gap staffing measures once word got out to the field about how bad things could be at headquarters—especially at CTD. Eighteen-month temporary duty staffing programs were put into place that offered opportunities for people to come to FBIHQ for financially beneficial short-term assignments. However, these programs only temporarily filled vacant positions to get Congress off of the leadership's back for requesting counterterrorism resources but not properly filling such sources in a timely fashion. FBIHQ began promoting people into vacant CTD leadership positions who probably should not have been there. Some people worked hard and learned, so this approach worked out in some instances. That said, these short-term staffing initiatives were largely a long-term failure.

There were sporadic instances of leaders who were effectively accomplishing the mission. But the focus on developing and sustaining the required mission capability, mentoring the people involved, marshaling resources effectively, and having genuine interest in the welfare of the CTD work teams started to slide to the wayside. The senior leadership environment changed to adopt managerial staffing practices that did not focus on recruiting or developing people with the right skills and attributes to fill the roles in support of the mission accomplishment and organizational character. In addition to the

CTD staffing and leadership challenges, significant changes were coming for other parts of the FBI—starting at FBIHQ and moving out to the field offices.

Deprioritized and Demoralized

As an example of the impact of September 11, 2001, on FBIHQ and field office programs, we should look at the Criminal Investigative Division (CID). Previously the FBI's flagship program. CID oversaw the formerly top-priority field programs for federal crime fighting. In broad terms, the CID and its programs were unceremoniously deprioritized post-2001 with CID staffing and funding being realigned (or raided, according to some people) to better equip the bureau's new top-priority national security programs. There would be no more FBI drug programs, truck-hijacking squads, or warrant squads. Bank robberies, once the domain of elite FBI investigators, were deprioritized and moved to state and local partners. Criminal investigative programs had to be reassessed and reformed to make do with the resources that were left. After the September 11th shift in program priority, the bureau saw its violent crime programs fall from being a top-tier priority to the number eight organizational priority (as of 2023).

While some of these organizational changes may have been necessary to cope with the prevailing national security threat environment, the FBI's criminal investigative cadre became demoralized and resentful. Many former criminal investigative special agents found themselves trying to involuntarily adjust to the new counterterrorism-focused investigative priorities. Many agents joined the FBI specifically to work in the criminal investigative programs, but they now were thrown into the classified world of national security. In this new world, no one was immediately being arrested (if ever), informants were not focused solely on locating and apprehending criminals, and agents were told to put their handcuffs away and integrate into the new FBI domestic intelligence and protective focus. As such, a major part of the organization was reeling from the violent shift in mission priority. To make things worse, a movement started on Capitol Hill where the national leadership contemplated dividing the FBI into two discrete organizations—one for criminal investigative work and the other for national security and intelligence work. This thought process added further insult and injury to an already demoralized FBI that was struggling to recover from the "intelligence failures" that supposedly led to the events of September 11, 2001.

The FBI's future was uncertain at this point, and Director Mueller, along with senior leadership, was working feverishly to preserve the bureau as a single, integrated organization. While Director Mueller was working to show that the FBI could successfully continue to operate in its blended crime fighting/national security configuration, he was also struggling to modernize legacy information technology systems, implement a new dedicated professional intelligence program to address identified gaps, and change the culture of the world's most respected law enforcement organization to that of an intelligence-led domestic security agency. Despite Director Mueller's efforts, the FBI remained a wounded apex predator in the Washington, DC, political jungle, and all of the previously lesser predators saw an opportunity to "help." It was time to settle old scores while trying to "help" the FBI make changes to its culture and practices.

> ## FILE REVIEW
>
> The value of true leadership cannot be overstated in managing an organization during and after a crisis situation. The modeling of behaviors and the training and mentoring offered by strong, capable leaders can build future generations of leaders. Law enforcement, national security, and other high-impact, high-stress, high-consequence missions cannot be successful with milquetoast leaders who are afraid to take on difficult matters, work hard, and occasionally kick a few tails to accomplish the mission. A balance between highly capable tactical leadership and insightful, forward-looking strategic leadership is required. While working through the pressure of a crisis and the immediate aftermath, organizational leaders must also consider the possible outcomes and possible undesired/unintended consequences of current mitigating actions. Organizational leaders must be able to determine possible negative effects that could harm people, assets, or infrastructures that comprise the organization's key operational resources. In addition, more esoteric factors can be damaged and must be protected as well, such as culture, trust, dedication, or pride. Again, making short-term fixes can cause longer-term strategic impacts. In this instance, FBIHQ decisions were made in a survival environment that caused organizational cultural declines in FBI investigative culture and special agent standing. Bottom line: good intentions do not always lead to good outcomes.

" The FBI was being directed to change its culture and legacy practices. "

8

GETTING BY WITH A LITTLE HELP FROM MY FRIENDS

This was a difficult time for the once mighty FBI, which was being assailed from all angles where the general feeling was that it could no longer do anything right. The FBI was being directed to change its culture and legacy practices by congressional leaders and was forced to accept (and pay for) external assistance from a private sector consultant firm (hereafter referred to as the "consultant") and various US intelligence community organizations. The consultant was invited into the bureau's inner workings by senior FBIHQ leaders to observe, assess, and render proposed courses of action that would help the bureau to "fix" itself. The FBI was largely considered "broken" due to the perception that it missed various investigative and intelligence cues that might have been useful in preventing the events of September 11, 2001.

While there was adequate failure and dysfunction throughout the US government, the FBI became the focus of much of the criticism that resulted from post-September 11th analyses and hearings. In its struggle to weather the storm, the bureau and its senior leadership became overly conciliatory and allowed various organizational practices and doctrines to be eroded, deprioritized, discouraged, or even discarded in line with the consultant's observations. Some sectors of the pre–September 11th FBI workforce felt abandoned with minimal support from their senior leaders. To make matters worse, at Director Mueller's instruction, a combined change management team, which included the consultant's representatives and hand-picked FBI personnel, was dubbed the Strategic Execution Team (SET) and foisted upon FBI field offices and investigative programs.

SET and the New FBI

SET was chartered to drive the FBI's move away from its reactive law enforcement culture and toward new intelligence-led, preventive domestic security operations. The SET initiative was charged with engaging with FBIHQ and field office personnel to spread the word about the change and to deliver Director Mueller's vision on what the "new FBI" would be doing and how it would conduct its mission.

In hindsight, the SET approach and its related culture change rollout were poorly formed and hastily executed. As such, the approach was initially met with cynicism, anxiety, and resentment among many FBIHQ and field office personnel. The first round of meetings at the Washington, DC, Field Office was characterized by reluctant acceptance, confusion, indifference, and hostility and was generally considered a train wreck. This unproductive change environment existed because FBIHQ provided a marginal change rollout program characterized by absent or limited communications with field office frontline and mid-level managers. This information vacuum caused an immediate disconnect due to rumors, fears, and bad information being passed throughout the organization before the SET personnel arrived. In addition, there was little to no active recruitment of mid-level FBI managers, which created a feeling of disenfranchisement and resulted in additional change resistance.

Many field office mid-level managers rejected the SET teams of FBI and consultant personnel, who struggled to answer basic questions or to address operational concerns. These SET teams extensively used private-sector jargon and business terminology that quickly lost their audiences, alienated tenured investigators, and led to arguments and poor interactions with field office personnel. The SET process was quickly caught in an adversarial environment of its own making, requiring a heavy hand from Director Mueller and FBIHQ senior leaders. FBIHQ would force the process and demand expedited compliance with new business principles and practices that very few people understood or wanted. What FBIHQ got was lukewarm compliance as opposed to invested performance, which is what the FBI really needed to be successful.

During the SET process, a cadre of agents, analysts, and professional staff members gained favor with FBIHQ senior leaders by supporting Director Mueller's objectives and SET party line. Certain SET FBI personnel and consultants (who were later hired as FBI employees) would ascend into influential roles that further changed the bureau's culture and moved it further from its roots. The SET initiative lasted several years and was eventually completed with varying degrees of success (depending on who you talked with). I watched this process unfold, and I knew many of the FBI personnel who were part of the initiative. They wanted to help the organization, but in many ways, they were sent on a fool's errand. SET was an example of how *not* to roll out and implement an organizational culture change. The SET initiative might deserve a separate case study to help future FBI leaders learn about the possible harm done to the foundational fiber and spirit of the organization.

A Groundwork for Challenges

From comments provided by FBI field office mid-level managers who were subjected to the SET initiative, I identified the following factors that contributed to why SET met with high resistance and low acceptance. Ultimately, the SET process produced questionable results that might not have enhanced FBI foundational practices but laid the early groundwork for some of the bureau's current challenges. The following observations may be applicable, in principle, to most any organizational change initiative.

- **Role ambiguity.** People were not clear on who was supposed to be doing what. People were questioning what would happen to their traditional roles and how they would fit into the "new FBI" according to SET. Many adjustments were made in how investigative supervisors would work with their newly established intelligence counterparts. The time of the special agent as the organization's primary leading role had ended, which caused more anxiety and uncertainty for the future.
- **Lack of mid-level manager stakeholder buy-in.** There was little to no recruitment of mid-level field office managers. From direct conversations and anecdotal recounts, very few people outside of the immediate SET organization could make sense of what was going on and they immediately took up defensive positions. Most agents in investigative leadership roles felt that the SET initiative was being forced on them, their careers were placed into jeopardy, and they were not even valued enough to be given the courtesy of an earnest conversation. People throughout the field

offices often felt uninformed, insulted, and betrayed and bucked the change process on principle alone.

- **Poorly executed change project roll-out.** Bad planning and execution all around. The SET initiative was rolled out too soon to meet arbitrary timelines. Many FBI investigative personnel felt that everything was premature and forced. There was insufficient connection and common perspective between the SET teams and traditional investigative leaders. A trusted friend and senior law enforcement professional once said to me: "If you want something bad, you will get it bad." FBIHQ badly wanted the SET initiative to proceed as quickly as possible, and it was badly done.
- **Forced change without proper orientation.** Many people did not understand what was going on with the SET initiative or why it was being implemented. As mentioned previously, communications were poor or non-existent, which led to anxiety and rumors. People largely did not even know what the expected outcomes of the initiative were. People were confused, felt threatened, and did not embrace (or even accept) the call for change. Most of the tenured FBI personnel merely complied with FBIHQ directives, which contributed to poor staff morale and facilitated the movement toward organizational mediocrity.
- **Lack of performance consultant credibility.** The consultants were seen as inexperienced interlopers. Many of them appeared to be younger (in their mid- to late-twenties or early thirties at best) with degrees from notable academic institutions. They were immediately disliked among the tenured FBI personnel who felt that they were being told what to do by young people with zero investigative experience and no credibility.

Some consultants insisted on using unfamiliar business jargon that caused them to appear arrogant or uninformed about how the bureau operated. Yet these consultants were there to "fix" the FBI. People did not buy it.

- **Inconsistent information and feedback.** Gaps in these areas allowed for rumors and fears to develop and fester. Communications were notably deficient before, during, and after the SET initiative. People often did not know what was going on or what was expected from them. When questions were asked of visiting SET representatives, many responses were canned or programmed, and people knew they were being given a party line. Many times, SET personnel could not answer questions and responded with "That is a build to…." That phrase became a joke across the organization. "Build to" became equated with "We do not know the answer…." "We do not have that part figured out yet…," or "We have no idea what we are doing…".

In addition to the organizational upheaval created by the SET initiative, managers from various US intelligence community (USIC) organizations were "detailed" to the FBI. They began filling various program management roles from line supervisory duties through the senior executive service (SES) ranks, which were just short of royalty at FBIHQ. The FBI rank and file saw USIC leaders come to FBIHQ, be placed into leadership positions, and try to import certain practices and principles from their respective parent agencies. Along with the SET initiative, the actions of the USIC detailees did not go over well in many instances. FBI personnel were being passed over for leadership opportunities and then insulted in many instances by being subjected to management by external USIC personnel. Some of the USIC personnel meant well, but they did not understand much, if anything, about FBI investigative policies, business practices, information management systems, or cultural attributes. Many simply did not care. For some USIC detailees, this was a chance to bring the FBI to heel. Director Mueller then created a new division-level intelligence program (modeled after the CIA's Directorate of Intelligence) and began staffing newly established intelligence analyst positions. The FBI's very own Directorate of Intelligence was born.

Other cultural and organizational changes taking place involved non-agent intelligence analysts immediately functioning as equals, if not superiors, to special agents. This was a major change for the FBI where special agents ruled supreme since its inception. This change caused short-term bad feelings and negatively affected the already low morale among FBI investigators. The question is not about whether the change was good or bad in a strategic sense but more about how this change was done and how it was received. The FBI's senior leaders did not consider how they might be creating an adversarial atmosphere that would have to be overcome. Many of agents did not want to speak openly due to fears of negative feedback or reprisal from FBI senior leaders, but their negative feelings were present nonetheless and were damaging to the core of organization.

Observational Experience

Regarding my own experience in working for a detailed USIC manager, I applied for a unit chief position (a mid-level manager role) to help build some of the newly commissioned CTD intelligence programs. These new programs were intended to shore up shortfalls in the FBI's ability to manage information in line with USIC practices and efficiently share raw field intelligence. I thought I could help by bringing my counterterrorism program experience to the new counterpart intelligence program. I also thought it would be interesting to help build it and to learn something new. I was fortunate to be selected for promotion to the unit chief position in the newly established CTD Terrorism Reports and Requirements Section (TRRS) where I would be working for a CIA analyst detailee. I would be leading a team comprised solely of intelligence analysts (no other special agents would be assigned to my unit).

This newly assembled intelligence team would be charged with developing and implementing new FBI intelligence processing and sharing processes. These processes would disseminate raw intelligence reporting for FBI field office consumption and USIC use in alignment with proven CIA methodologies for their own field operators. I was excited about my new role, as I would be leading an expanded team in an emergent program. I also looked forward to resolving an identified shortfall in the FBI's national security practices. I looked at this opportunity as a new way to provide a service for my CTD colleagues because I knew how things were done in CTD, and I could easily integrate new intelligence program efforts with my former CTD colleagues.

The CIA analyst detailee I would be working for occupied an FBI section chief position (an entry-level executive role) and was initially characterized as a tenured, highly capable intelligence professional. When my promotion was formally approved and publicized, I made an appointment to introduce myself to my new CIA detailee boss. I was met with a surprising (and disappointing) introductory discussion. At the beginning of our meeting, the CIA detailee section chief said hello and then proceeded to speak poorly about the FBI.

She then told me that I should not think I was any better than my soon-to-be assigned intelligence analyst staff members because I was a special agent. I was a bit surprised with the tone of the conversation, and I advised her that I did not believe that I was better than anyone. I also said that I looked forward to working with and learning from the intelligence analysts. The CIA detailee merely said that she hoped so, and our first meeting was unceremoniously over.

This person's overt disdain for the FBI, its practices, and special agents was present from day one and in various future meetings. It was also made clear in various discussions with her throughout my TRRS assignment. While I was fortunate to work with some outstanding intelligence analysts during this assignment, the time spent working for this CIA detailee taught me volumes about how organizational cultures, values, and practices could clash. Her disposition and personal feelings about the FBI affected the people and operations under her watch. She was a career CIA analyst, but she had absolutely no knowledge about how the FBI conducted investigations, and she could not care less. Because she could be an inconsiderate and critical taskmaster, I also learned about the importance of protecting my staff members from unearned scrutiny from higher organizational levels while I helped them to learn and perform in the most positive, productive, and professional work environment I could provide.

I had a great team of smart, dedicated intelligence analysts, and we did some good work together. I enjoyed working with them, and I refined my leadership approaches to build relationships with people of various ages, experience sets, and worldviews. Besides this super group of analysts, there was one other person who was a saving grace in this assignment: my assistant section chief (ASC), an FBI agent who, thankfully, served as my immediate supervisor. The ASC was the nominal second-in-command of our intelligence section and was a source of common sense and professionalism when the CIA detailee was inflicting pain and suffering on her staff.

The ASC was a friendly, even-tempered person who served as a buffer between the CIA detailee and the work force. He showed me that we did not have to like our boss, but we had to support her and do a good job for the FBI. He gave me insights about properly representing the bureau with people from outside the organization and for taking accountability for all FBI-related issues when one of us was the sole FBI representative in various interagency meetings. He told me that we were not just there for TRRS business when attending interagency meetings, but we were also representing the FBI and its interests. He was my sounding board when I would get fed up with the antics and poor behavior of the CIA detailee. He would listen, let me blow off steam, and let me come to my own conclusions without judgment. The ASC was a good person, a sanity-saver in many instances, and I enjoyed working with him.

Despite the great people I was fortunate to work with, I was glad to finish this assignment and watch the CIA detailee leave the FBI. I tried hard to not hold her attitude and managerial performance against the entire CIA—at least not too much.

FILE REVIEW

I learned that it was my job to maintain a measured response to workplace activities and act as a bullshit barrier for my staff members who were working hard to execute their duties and responsibilities in an already challenging work environment. I had to be mentally harder and emotionally stronger as a leader, and I had to sustain thick skin for the disdain that my USIC detailee often displayed for the FBI and for special agents. It was not about me, and I did not have to like my boss, but I did have to do a good job in support of the mission. I learned to absorb negativity and to protect my people from that garbage (and not to display any similar poor behavior). I also learned (or was reminded) that I represented the entire FBI wherever I went and whoever I was with (especially in interagency meetings). No matter the subject at hand, my responsibility as an agent and organizational leader was to protect the FBI, its people, and its interests at all times.

"Give people a chance to recover from a bad day and not have to worry about having their asses kicked."

9

WASHINGTON FIELD OFFICE, WASHINGTON D.C.

I completed my initial FBIHQ tour with the culmination of my TRRS assignment and was selected as a squad supervisor at the FBI's Washington, DC, Field Office (WFO) within the office's Counterintelligence Division. I felt fortunate to be working in the FBI's Counterintelligence Program where I could expand my experience bases and oversee clandestine technical operations along with sensitive human intelligence initiatives against the US government's primary international adversaries and competitors.

The Importance of Patience

For my first field office squad supervisor role, I would be working with a team of highly experienced senior agents who comprised an exceptional cadre of investigators and counterintelligence operators. I was at a notable disadvantage as they were my superiors in operational knowledge, experience, and organizational standing (similar to my CTD assignment with Bonnie and Clyde). I immediately began receiving briefings on prevailing threats, priorities, and operating practices and saw even more clearly how much I had to learn. I was moving into an operating environment outside of the counterterrorism world, and I would be pushed to adapt my prior experiences to the tasks at hand and see where I had knowledge gaps that had to be prioritized and filled.

The only advantage I had (in my mind) was that I held an organizational designation as a supervisor. While I acclimated to my new operating environment and program requirements, I learned a great deal about how to conduct and manage technical special operations from my senior agent teammates. I immediately saw how these types of "dark side" operations were essential (and in some instances indispensable) to our ability to protect US interests from hostile nation-state adversaries—both at home and abroad. We worked closely with other US government agencies and conducted sophisticated counterintelligence operations against our top-tier adversaries. This was the kind of work that was highlighted in movies and TV shows.

This was an enjoyable and educational tour of duty. My senior agent team members were kind enough to take me under their experienced wings and help me to mature as an FBI supervisory special agent. Many of the team members were old breed special agents, and it felt good to be among more traditional agents again. In this environment, I learned about the importance of patience (still not one of my primary virtues), and I relearned how to work with people who were better at everything than I was—despite the fact that I was nominally in charge.

I recall one instance when I learned that having patience was the best way to navigate an interpersonal situation that could have gone very badly (but luckily did not). I was talking with a senior special agent on my squad who was not having a good day. I had to talk with her about an operational matter that she was strongly opposed to. After I presented the matter at hand, this senior agent explained to me, in colorful assertive detail, that she was "KMA" and that she did not have to put up with any of that nonsense. (The language was cleaned up for this book, but she was rather animated at the time.) I had heard the term KMA before. It stands for "kiss my ass," which is what many senior agents say when they become retirement eligible and supposedly stop caring as much. I knew that this person was not having a great day as she was a superior special agent and a professional from the old breed of agents. So, I decided to move the conversation to other topics (which I probably would not have done earlier in the more linear part of in my career). I told her that I have my own definition of what KMA means. She asked what that might be. I responded with "kick my ass," meaning that she needed a kick in the behind to get rid of her bad attitude. She started laughing and said she had not heard that before, and she thanked me for the laugh. We talked a bit more and then this consummate professional went out, dealt with the difficult people she did not care for, and did what she did not want to do—and did it all exceptionally well. All it took was a bit of patience and appreciation for this senior agent's concerns as I provided a pass for her bad day. I tried to employ this approach wherever I could in later parts of my career to give people a chance to recover from a bad day and not have to worry about having their asses kicked.

I learned in this and in other similar situations that a bit of patience, a sense of humor, and understanding can resolve a lot of issues and tough spots. This was what I always liked best about the old breed senior agents—they could usually be counted on to hold the mission first and keep personal feelings second. As a point of reference, the senior special agent in this situation and her partner case agent (who was also a fine special agent but not as tenured) later won the FBI director's award for technical advancement due to their operational excellence and achievement in an undercover operation against hostile international intelligence adversaries. I developed the highest respect and admiration for these outstanding senior special agents. Their accomplishments in the shadow world of counterintelligence would never receive the recognition they deserved in their service to our nation. They knew that and did it all anyway.

While I learned a great deal about the counterintelligence field from investigative and operational perspectives, my most important benefit was the improvement in my interpersonal skills. I became more patient with people while planning and executing field operations. I also refined my ability to lead and work with those who were better than I was at most everything. Coming from the somewhat different and more intense counterterrorism field, I improved my tolerance for the working methods and working paces of others when conducting the covert operations that protect our country in places that remain hidden and unfamiliar to most. Unfortunately, many other activities and learning opportunities from this assignment cannot be discussed in this book due to the classifications and operating sensitivities surrounding our accomplishments.

The world of counterintelligence is complex. Great competitions are waged in a world that most people are unaware of, and it is probably better that way. This is a world of endeavor without a lot of fanfare or recognition of accomplishment. I developed the mindset that quietly doing a good job for the right reasons was sometimes its only reward.

I salute all of the people I was privileged to work with on this assignment. While I was working with you, I knew that the world was a better and safer place due to your professionalism, personal efforts, and ability to firmly put foot to ass for our nation. I can only hope that you trained and mentored our successors in that same careful, thoughtful way that you helped me to be successful.

Learning to Lead Other Leaders

While still assigned to the WFO Counterintelligence Program, I received a promotion to an assistant special agent in charge (ASAC) position for the WFO Mission Support Division. In this role, I concurrently served as the WFO chief security officer, head of technical and undercover services, facility supervisor for the Northern Virginia Resident Agency Building, and ad-hoc manager of various administrative processes (as determined by mission needs). This was a highly educational tour of duty for me, as I learned about the FBI administrative and business programs that supported investigations and enabled operations. The ASAC role is usually a gateway to higher level FBI leadership opportunities, so this was an important role. I was fortunate to be promoted into a business area in which I learned and grew in administrative functions that later helped me to better navigate the FBI corporate machine and teach my staff members how to do the same.

These administrative functions I was now involved with included programs such as finance, hiring, human resources, procurement, facilities, policy development, compliance, logistics, and security. Previously, I had been involved primarily in investigative and technical operations, so I was fairly familiar with investigations and operational security measures, but I had a lot to learn about the business side of the FBI. This position was also a large jump in supervisory scope, so I had to adjust my leadership approach to match the expanded scope of responsibility. I now had a staff of approximately 190 people who covered a wide range of roles and programs (a marked increase from my previous squad of fifteen).

I began to learn how to be a leader of leaders because I had squad supervisors (which was my previous position) who were now my direct report staff members. Based upon the maturity of the people involved, I found many instances in which instruction and influence worked better than straight command and control to reach objectives and expected outcomes. I became a better problem-solver and collaborator with my fellow ASACs to effectively manage the considerable workforce and resources of the WFO. At the time, WFO had fifteen ASAC mid-level managers to oversee the 1,800 people and significant resource bases assigned to the office. WFO was (and remains) the second largest FBI field office after the New York office. I also figured out how to better control my own ego and interests while focusing more on mission objectives, organizational needs, and personnel welfare on all levels. I worked with and supervised clerical personnel, special agents, and supervisory special agents, and I built relationships with people throughout the office with various backgrounds, experience levels, and value systems. I had no problem working with and supporting other program personnel and leaders. I began the development of an "enterprise service provider" mentality that further helped to keep my ego and personal feelings out of business decisions as much as possible. I enjoyed my time as a large office ASAC.

My ASAC assignment was going well (at least I thought so). I made some significant logistical and process-based improvements that brought me into the good graces of the office's senior leaders. I developed good relationships with my ASAC peers and the squad supervisors who worked in my assigned programs. I thought I had arrived as an FBI field office mid-level manager, and I began to think that I was a fairly capable leader and manager. Little did I know that my next assignment would be a defining point in my career (and a swift kick in the behind). This next assignment would show me how much more I had to learn to be even a decent FBI leader and a moderately effective operations manager.

After I had been at the WFO for several years, I decided to apply for a promotion into the senior executive service (SES) managerial program, which was the next echelon of leadership in the federal government. While looking at possible FBI job postings, I saw a vacancy posting for a position at the Terrorist Screening Center (TSC) as the deputy director for operations. The TSC was a relatively new counterterrorism-related program within the FBI's National Security Branch. I thought I would be competitive based on my previous counterterrorism operations experience along with my ASAC experience at WFO. I thought I was a competent leader of people and programs at this point. But I was wrong yet again. I was going to painfully learn what I was lacking and what I would need to be an effective leader of people, programs, and systems at the Terrorist Screening Center.

Moving Forward

I applied for the TSC SES position, and I was fortunate to be selected for an interview. I did some preparatory research and, since I did not know anyone who worked at the TSC, I only found some surface-level information on the TSC's web page on the FBI Intranet. As noted previously, the TSC was a relatively new FBI national security component and was operated as a multi-agency center that provided government-wide services and products for global counterterrorism watchlisting and screening. The TSC was created circa 2003 as a primary member of a network that consolidated and unified worldwide counterterrorism interdiction operations. As part of its duty set, the TSC served as a twenty-four-hour primary protective element for the entire US government. That was all I knew about the TSC when I showed up for my candidate interview. I walked into a conference room full of at least twelve people, and this is when I met the sitting TSC director (who will be referred to as "Harrier"). I would find Harrier to be a hyper-focused, high-energy, intense leader who was a stickler for detail, thoroughness, and sharp execution in all things. He demanded immense effort from his managers and staff members, had a strong personality, and could be very intimidating for the faint of heart. Harrier was a former US Marine Corps officer and aviator, so maybe that is where he gained his strong appreciation for operational excellence and proper execution in all things.

After the interview with Harrier and his team, I left feeling that it did not go very well. I then set my sights on other entry-level SES jobs that might be available. A few weeks later, I received a surprising notification that I had been selected for the TSC deputy director position. Once I recovered from the shock, I began developing a transition plan to leave my WFO ASAC position and move into the new TSC operations leader role. I was looking forward to immediately being a mission contributor, leader, and asset to the TSC. I thought I was ready for this new assignment with the leadership skill set and experience that I had gained. As noted earlier and as usual, I was wrong.

FILE REVIEW

My experiences to this point became learning opportunities that helped me change some of my thoughts on leadership and to develop more refined views on working with people of different backgrounds and beliefs. I saw that organizations of all sizes are made up of individuals who have unique strengths, limitations, values, practices, and life experiences. Becoming a beneficial leader requires being receptive to other perspectives while being mature enough to learn from other staff members and colleagues. I grew into the understanding that organizational leaders must have confidence but must avoid becoming prideful, especially when subordinates, colleagues, or adversaries have superior skills. I learned that it could be extremely difficult to be a competent leader without striving to be better than everyone at everything.

In my leadership development experience, two of my formal FBI leadership roles were defined by being nominally in charge of people who were better than I was at everything. I had been given position power as a manager, but I had to learn how to be a good leader among colleagues and staff members. Stated simply, position power does not allow a new leader to lead a highly experienced, tenured staff for long. I had to ask for help from the people I was supposedly in charge of to learn how things worked. I also worked on forming relationships, helping team members to build confidence in me and each other, and letting my teams come to know me as a competent, dependable, trustworthy leader.

While I was in charge and had authority, I scarcely used that type of direct influence. It could often have been the easier path, but it was also the least effective in the long term. As such, I began asking (not directing) people to complete tasks and obtain outcomes. I then explained why we were doing things. When making plans, I shared ideas and asked for feedback, as much as possible. As a result, I rarely had to give an order because I was blessed with highly capable, responsible teammates who knew what to do and how to do it. My job was to give the reasons why we were doing things, watch for conflicts, resolve coordination issues, and sort out procedural challenges. I was no longer doing the actual job, but I was, instead, supporting and assisting the people doing it. Later in my executive career, I provided this same support and assistance to the leaders who were supporting the people doing the job.

These relatively simple dynamics tend to be the source of leadership challenges and often become the areas where most organizations fail their people. Senior leaders must learn to guide operations and facilitate developmental opportunities for people, teams, and intermediate leaders so that the mission is accomplished. Senior leaders must ensure that a culture and workplace environment exist where all team members can do their respective jobs, treat each other with dignity and tact, and skillfully accomplish the mission. Senior leaders must minimize the negative effects of unchecked ego and turf battles while they maximize thoughtful, competent leadership. If this can be done, most other things in the workplace tend to sort themselves out.

"I worked hard, and I learned how to manage projects and programs with greater precision and insight."

10

TERRORIST SCREENING CENTER, NATIONAL SECURITY BRANCH

My move from field office operations to the TSC was a strange and humbling experience. It was vastly different from the traditional FBI case-based investigative and operations environment I was familiar with. The TSC was created to address certain US government security and information management deficiencies that were identified in the post-event analysis of the September 11th tragedy. I immediately found the TSC to be unique in that it operated on a set of business principles and information management processes that had more in common with the private sector than with traditional FBI case management processes. I would later learn that this mode of operation set the TSC apart from other FBI operational and intelligence components.

Reporting for TSC Duty—A Somewhat Rude Awakening

When I reported to the center for my first duty day, I met with Harrier. He was intense, as usual, and he gave me a short overview about the working state of the TSC's mission, programs, and business practices. This was when I found out that he was the center's first deputy director for operations

(DD-Ops), and that he personally built, established, and oversaw the formation of most of the center's programs. Harrier told me that he expected me to hit the ground sprinting—not just running—because he did not have time for that. Then he smiled and told me that he was glad that I was there and that he expected me to do my job, and if I did not do it to his satisfaction, he would do it for me. He asked me if I had any questions. I had none for him, but I was seriously asking myself what the hell I was doing there. Honestly, I was not sure I was up to the task. I left a good comfortable situation at WFO, and I was not sure that I made the right choice in moving to the TSC. But like the assignment to my first training agent in Newark, this was a blessing in disguise.

Over the next several months, Harrier was a more fearsome taskmaster than I had experienced to date. While he was tough, he taught me how to lead and manage in a stressful, no-compromise operations environment. I often felt inadequate and out of position because he knew my job better than I did—after all, he built most everything at the TSC. So, I worked hard, and I learned how to manage projects and programs with greater precision and insight. I had to improve rapidly because Harrier demanded 360-degree program manager awareness and accountability during his periodic strategic performance sessions, where he personally assessed center health, welfare, and achievement. Most people across the center feared and dreaded these sessions due to the intense scrutiny and program micro-examination. During these organizational performance evaluations, Harrier would review everything and evaluate the state of operations and business management across the center. The first few sessions where I had to present my programs were comparable to an excruciating root canal combined with any other highly undesirable form of torturous, invasive medical procedure you can think of. Once again, these sessions were blessings in disguise. By attending and participating in these sessions, I became familiar with Harrier's expectations. I also began to understand TSC programs in detail and could identify the root causes for operating difficulties. Most importantly, I started to become predictive and anticipatory in looking for program challenges and possible shortfalls as a way to stay ahead of Harrier. I took this new perspective with me for the rest of my FBI career.

Learning from a Tough Leader— The Quick and the Dead

To survive and learn quickly, I formed beneficial relationships with fellow managers and staff members, as I was unfamiliar with TSC operations and business practices. My initial grace period with Harrier ended within a few hours of my arrival at the TSC, so I had to move fast to prove my value or suffer marginalization as Harrier drove operations forward. I had to be quick to learn or my career would be dead. I studied Harrier as a leader and started to understand his thought processes, which allowed me to anticipate his preferences, needs, and concerns. Eventually, I learned about the threat environment and the center's programs, and I began proposing or making process/practice changes to sharpen processes, remove self-imposed obstacles, and fill performance gaps. Soon, I could answer almost any question Harrier had about center operations, and I was getting better at anticipating his preferences. I had to extend myself further than I had at any point in my FBI career just to keep up—but I started to keep up and sometimes get ahead of Harrier.

Harrier gradually grew to trust and confide in me. He eventually gave me the authority to run center operations, intelligence programs, and administrative functions on his behalf. As we built our relationship, I knew these were not my programs—they clearly belonged to Harrier—but I took ownership as if they were mine. I protected my staff members from his intensity and occasional wrath and got my staff members in front of him to brief on program successes and achievements. I owned all program shortcomings, and Harrier's confidence grew in me and in my mid-level managers. He began stepping back and functioning on a more strategic level now that he had a leadership team that worked together and that he trusted (for the most part).

Looking back, I can honestly say that this was the toughest but most educational and developmental tour of duty in my FBI career. I must give recognition to two people who devoted many hours of their time to teach me how things worked at the TSC: George and Gracie, who were contractors working on Harrier's personal process review team. They were in-house gurus on the programs and systems that comprised the center's mission capability. George and Gracie were gracious and patient in tutoring me almost daily on the TSC's essential processes as it executed its global security mission. They were exceedingly smart and authoritative while I was the epitome of mediocrity, but I worked hard to learn and absorb what they shared. As I learned from them, I eventually became more capable, and I began proving myself as being capable of leading people and managing assets and infrastructures at the TSC. I could not have been successful without the mentorship, friendship, and circle of trust that George and Gracie provided.

Insights Learned

During my time at the TSC, Harrier and my operational leaders and staff members helped me to balance my perspectives in essential business areas that had not been prioritized in the FBI's more traditional investigative environment (which, in hindsight, was a corporate FBI shortfall). The TSC and its impressive operations cadre supported me in improving my capability in the following areas, which carried me for the rest of my career:

- Strategic and tactical planning
- Formulation of goals and objectives
- Program metrics
- Performance measurement and monitoring
- Systems analysis
- Problem-solving
- Program integration
- Budget formulation
- Action plans
- Interagency operations
- Staff engagement and involvement
- Information technology management
- Team building

My assignment at the TSC formed the new baseline for many of my enduring leadership practices. I believed that many of the bureau's programs could have benefited greatly from emulating applicable TSC business and operational approaches. However, the FBI's program managers outside the TSC resisted the adoption of these superior business practices. As I would find out, organizational hubris, along with the egos of many program managers and senior leaders would lead to a host of organizational challenges over the next several years.

FILE REVIEW

I thought I was a fairly capable leader upon my arrival at the TSC, but I was sorely mistaken. I had much to learn and do that the FBI had not prepared me for in terms of leadership and management skills. Having proper leadership and organizational management training can substantially enhance a person's chances of being successful when entering onto executive leadership duty; however, being placed into such a role will not guarantee that the required skills will manifest or be further developed. I depended on a strong support system to gain the necessary skills to become even remotely successful. While many organizational mechanics can be added for separate discussion and debate, I will summarize two important leadership concepts that helped to guide my macro decision-making and to keep me on the right track:

1. **Being Accountability-Based:** A culture of accountability must be developed and sustained. Accountability has become an overused word with many meanings, but I will share my personal definition: *Doing what is expected in line with mission accomplishment, every time, even when no one is watching. Bottom line —Are you doing what you are supposed to be doing and are you doing what you say you are doing?* Low accountability often leads to low confidence. Low confidence leads to micromanagement and then to poor organizational effectiveness, staff turnover, and lack of initiative. Everyone loses.

2. **Being Results-Oriented:** Are desired results being attained in a timely manner, in line with expected outcomes and mission objectives? Obtaining results by marshaling people and resources is the ultimate responsibility for leaders; however, our society has become overly fixated on feelings rather than performance in getting the job done. Leaders must provide an environment in which people are treated with dignity and tact, are given proper resources and training, and are provided with clear mission objectives and the "why" of the tasks at hand. No matter how happy staff members might be, the leader must attain organizational objectives. Failure to focus on targeted results will waste time and resources, use up goodwill with people, and lead to failure. Everyone loses again.

"The office was missing a sense of warriorship in its operations, and I saw a lack of finesse when planning sensitive operations."

11

SPECIAL-AGENT-IN-CHARGE, BUFFALO, NEW YORK, FIELD OFFICE

I was making strides at the TSC and felt that I had significantly improved my leadership and management skills, so I talked with Harrier about my next career steps. I decided to return to field operations and apply for a promotion to the role of special-agent-in-charge (SAC), who serves as the chief executive for all related investigations, operations, and business activities in an FBI field office. As a matter of background, the bureau maintains fifty-six field offices across the US (including Alaska, Hawaii, and Puerto Rico). Each office covers a geographic area where it investigates federal crime problems, national security matters, cyber threats, and other matters of federal jurisdiction. Harrier supported my efforts, and my promotion application was accepted and reviewed by the FBIHQ SES Career Board. When career board deliberations were completed, I was fortunate to be promoted by the FBI director to serve as the SAC of the Buffalo, New York, Field Office.

The Buffalo Field Office was one of the FBI's smaller medium-sized offices, located far from the TSC and Washington, DC—not just geographically but also in operational culture, as I was about to find out. When I was officially announced as the new SAC for the Buffalo Field Office, I received a call from a friend working in human resources who congratulated me. He then laughingly told me that Buffalo was the bureau's worst-performing field office in its personnel timekeeping and reporting compliance, a performance metric tracked by the director's office. He said I should "get right on that." I thanked him (crassly) for the backhanded congratulatory call, and I made a note to look into this compliance issue. Aside from this type of administrative oversight, I would serve as the chief executive for all Buffalo Field Office investigative, business, and liaison matters. I was hoping that the office was doing all right in all other areas outside of timekeeping. As usual, I was wrong.

The Challenges of Being in Charge

Upon reporting to the Buffalo Field Office in July 2011, I spent most evenings during my first couple of weeks reading inspection interrogatories, which were FBIHQ Inspection Division program assessment documents. Buffalo was scheduled for a program review, which took a lot of time and effort to prepare for and execute properly. While painful for me in some respects, it was a chance to jump into the deep end of the field office leadership pool. This course of action forced me to grab on tightly and become familiar with the office I would now be leading. FBIHQ program inspections are a big deal and can make or break field offices and their management teams. This internal auditing program ensures that FBI offices are operating effectively and efficiently and in compliance with all FBI requirements.

In reading the Buffalo inspection interrogatories, I immediately encountered varying levels of mission disconnect, apathy, and cultural distance from what was going on at FBIHQ. I was FBI inspection-certified and was a designated inspector-in-place, so I knew that the information I was reviewing could bring a storm of scrutiny from FBIHQ. From my initial contact with my new field office, I could see that the sitting senior leadership had slid into an overly relaxed sense of urgency. The office, as a whole, showed a low level of mission ownership and prioritized action. The atmosphere I encountered in Buffalo was almost the direct opposite of the TSC. The TSC was intense and squared away in most respects, and it maintained a high operational tempo with a strong culture of organizational mission ownership. The Buffalo Field Office did not display any of these characteristics when I arrived.

As the new SAC, my arrival at the Buffalo Field Office was met with general indifference, and the office senior leaders did not appear to be particularly concerned about making a good impression. Let me be clear—I was not expecting anyone to lay out a red carpet or to provide pomp and circumstance (which I dislike anyway), but I was looking for some baseline professionalism when it came to the state of mission capability, the general office atmosphere, and the maintenance of the office facilities and assets. I found that the Buffalo office was soft in these areas (and others, as I would find out), and I set about to provide the leadership team with my expectations and to begin making some foundational changes.

I found that Buffalo had fallen into a slow, almost lackadaisical approach to operations. I encountered insufficient organizational mission integration as many people were doing their own thing, some were going through the motions, and others were doing little to nothing at all. I had a lot of ground to cover, so I began reviewing and updating the program practices to promote a more business-like approach and an FBI approach. I also implemented structured, regular interactions with the entire supervisory staff to reinforce my expectations for our next several years together.

As an example of the lax office culture that I encountered, the Buffalo Field Office's acting SAC did not think I would read the inspection interrogatories that were ready for submission to FBIHQ. As the new SAC, I was not officially responsible for the office's state of operation until about ninety days after my arrival. The acting SAC felt that the inspection submissions were in good shape, but I knew that a self-inflicted disaster was coming if the inspection package was submitted in the form I saw.

All field offices received inspection interrogatories that the program supervisors would fill out. These interrogatories would be evaluated by FBIHQ inspectors for program performance, best practices, and deficiencies. Too many deficiencies or a few high-impact deficiencies found during the inspection process could be grounds for the punitive removal of sitting field office leaders. I observed this firsthand when I was assigned to the Newark Field Office earlier in my career. In that instance, the Newark SAC and most of the ASACs were summarily removed by Director Freeh for questionable leadership and management practices that he became aware of during one of his field office visits. Most everyone in FBI channels knew that field office inspections, while a necessary evil, were labor-intensive, time-consuming, and disruptive. A poor inspection showing could have a negative impact on the autonomy of the office and to people's career aspirations. That said, the sitting Buffalo Field Office senior managers were mistaken about my willingness to spend most evenings during my first couple of weeks reviewing and editing the office's inspection interrogatory content. This kind of in-depth program review was regular business from my previous life at the TSC.

Buffalo was now my field office—ninety-day grace period or not—and I had been entrusted with its mission, staff, assets, and programs. So, I would read the program interrogatories and review every program response submission, most of which required extensive upgrading and rewriting. While most of the Buffalo inspection write-ups were weak and incomplete, I learned from conversations with squad supervisors and program managers that the office was actually doing better work than was being reported to the Inspection Division. During these conversations, I found that the program supervisors had a better understanding of the office's prevailing threat and operating environments, available human capital, and investigative capabilities/capacities than the program write-ups conveyed. I spoke with the program supervisors and provided proposed edits to their inspection submissions, asking them to clearly articulate their program activities and achievements. When I asked why incomplete information was initially included in the documents, most of the supervisors simply gave me blank stares and uncertain responses. This was an oversight failure by the office's ASACs who should have set and monitored standards to help their program supervisors be mission-focused and engaged. I filed these conversations away in my mind to decide later if these supervisors simply did not know how to function during an inspection or if they just did not care—or maybe both.

A Changing Culture

I told a few of the office's line supervisors that their investigative areas appeared to be lagging due to a lack of mission focus and discipline in their inspection write-ups. I explained that weakly assembled inspection interrogatories that lacked substance and appropriate ownership would be seen by

FBIHQ as deficient and would draw corrective attention and scrutiny, which we could all do without.

After this exercise, I found that the Buffalo operations culture had inconsistent levels of discipline with mediocre planning and lukewarm execution. There was apparently little to no sense of urgency or purpose in most programs, and I found what I considered a compliance-based environment instead of a performance-based environment. As such, people around the office tended to do only what was required to meet minimum requirements, to stay out of trouble, or to keep their supervisors off of their backs. The office was missing a sense of warriorship in its operations, and I saw a lack of finesse when planning sensitive operations.

As an example of a shortfall in finesse, shortly after I arrived at the Buffalo Field Office, I was advised of a planned arrest operation. As the result of a public corruption investigation, one of the white-collar crime squads would be making an arrest at Buffalo city hall of an administrative employee who had made some bad choices with city financial resources. I thought this was a good opportunity to find out how the office conducted such operations. What I heard was kind of surprising and somewhat disappointing.

The office's criminal program ASAC and the white-collar program supervisor stated that they intended to enter the city hall unannounced, wearing FBI raid jackets, and make the arrest during the business day. I asked about coordination with the mayor's office and the Buffalo police commissioner, and I was advised that there was none. The ASAC and the supervisor felt that the mayor might have been accused of his own corruption allegations, and they did not want to alert him. They also did not want to alert the Buffalo police commissioner because they thought he would alert the mayor.

After listening to this explanation, I told the ASAC and supervisor that I could not support or authorize such a course of action. I saw no benefit from FBI bravado in wearing raid jackets to arrest an administrative worker at city hall. I knew I had to discuss this matter with the Buffalo police commissioner, despite the concerns of my staff members. I told the ASAC and supervisor that I would not put the commissioner in such a situation with the mayor and that I believed withholding such information was less than professional. The Buffalo police commissioner was supposed to be one of our closest law-enforcement allies, and we could not simply leave him hanging. I agreed that we would not contact the mayor directly. I called the commissioner, explained the matter at hand, and laid out our plan. We would enter quietly (with no raid jackets). With his and the mayor's assistance, we would take custody of the employee in a low-key, controlled fashion and would depart city hall without incident. The commissioner thanked me for the call and then briefed the mayor on a "his-ears-only" basis on what was planned. The commissioner then called me back, thanking me for the opportunity to brief the mayor, who also expressed gratitude for the notification and for taking such a professional approach. The commissioner relayed the mayor's intent to support and help us whenever needed. The arrest was made without incident and with no fanfare, no raid jackets, and no problems.

Our agents did a good job, and the mayor and commissioner were happy with the outcome. City Hall used the incident to highlight their desire to root out corrupt behavior. In the aftermath, I received a call from the commissioner, who said that he appreciated having the opportunity to manage the situation with the mayor. The commissioner's personal stock rose significantly with the mayor, and all was good.

Throughout my time in Buffalo, the commissioner became one of my strongest law-enforcement allies. We worked together—through our highly capable agents and officers, of course—to make a measurable 20 percent reduction in gang-related crime. The Buffalo office maintained a cordial relationship with the mayor's office, and we went on to work with the city in a few other white-collar criminal matters. In the end, we took the "old" FBI way that I was taught by the old breed agents—professional, quiet, and effective.

As I reflected on this matter, I was stunned by the tone and approach of the initial arrest plans, and I believed that the American people deserved better than that kind of business model from the FBI. In addition to the operational attitudes among my staff members, I saw that personal relationships seemed to dominate managerial decision-making across the Buffalo Field Office. These relationships often appeared to hold more importance than the objective prioritization of mission capability and investigative program requirements. The following rather silly situation introduced me to the personal relationship–driven business environment that I would later find throughout the office.

At one point, I tried to call the Resident Agency (RA) in Rochester, New York, but no one answered the telephone. The Rochester RA was a large satellite office out of the Buffalo Field Office that covered investigative and operational responsibilities for that geographic area. I thought that the lack of answer at the RA was odd, and I asked the administrative officer (AO) how the Rochester RA covered its telephones in case of an emergency. The AO looked pained and then explained that the two people who covered all of the incoming calls at that office did not like each other and refused to answer each other's phones if one wasn't available. I was stupefied. How could we do business that way and leave our primary communications in such a state of dysfunction? Here we were, the FBI, all but unreachable in one of western New York's largest cities due to an office feud. I instructed the AO to resolve the situation immediately—the personal disconnect between those two people must end because it was causing our RA to be unreachable. I further explained that administrative field office leaders must actively seek out and resolve such conflicts that reduced our operational availability and effectiveness. She quickly took care of the matter (as she did for everything I asked her to do), but I wondered how business in the office got to that point.

Over time, I witnessed other instances in which personal relationships and the desire to be liked by others had an excessive impact on office business. On several instances, I had to counsel some of the supervisors due to personal business being more important than bureau business. I wondered how business was being conducted in other field offices. I also wondered how the FBI was protecting its communities if the type of lax, personality-driven field office environment I encountered in Buffalo existed elsewhere. (We will find this to be the case in a later discussion about an Indianapolis Field Office investigative debacle.) I later found that this ridiculous situation was representative of other challenges in the Buffalo office. I knew that improvements had to be made on many levels—and they would be.

I felt that allowing people to make jobs "their own" was good to a certain level but letting office business drift into being personality-driven could be damaging to the organization's mission, goals, and objectives. When leaders allowed personal preferences, relationships, and agendas to take precedence over mission requirements, operations suffered and friendships and fiefdoms began to rule the day. In addition, I saw instances where leaders became more interested in being liked versus being respected and effective. While I wanted to facilitate a friendly. comfortable workplace, I had no interest in any kind of frat house or adult daycare environment to form, as these defective environments are difficult to correct. I expected Buffalo leaders to be honest and objective in letting their staff members know that no one person's point of view or personal preferences are more important than the fundamental reason that the organization exists.

Purpose and Mission Priority

The Buffalo Field Office needed a sense of purpose and mission priority, so I proceeded to recruit line supervisors into my desired business models. I coached program managers into assessing their programs and suggesting changes. I encouraged the two ASACs to strengthen their program engagement and personnel management approaches. I required sharper program execution, so I held the ASACs more accountable in reporting how their programs were performing (or not).

I worked closely with the AO who was the lead non-agent manager in the field office. She was excellent, and she effectively managed the multiple concurrent business activities that kept the office running. She sharpened field office business management practices and worked with me to improve and update various office processes and fill facility needs.

Based on my previous TSC experience, I instituted periodic program reviews and reporting sessions to give supervisors a chance to speak directly with me to highlight their program achievements. I wanted them to recognize the hard work and accomplishments of their people, to take personal responsibility for shortfalls, and to explain how we would recover from or mitigate such shortfalls for future operations. During these meetings, I introduced programmatic instructions, provided feedback, and reinforced program expectations. I repeatedly highlighted requirements for professionalism, supervisory execution and follow-up, and staff member performance management. I told the supervisors that we were going to become the FBI field office that we should be and that the American people deserved. And we did.

Over the next couple of years, I worked with the Buffalo ASACs and the administrative officer to rehabilitate underperforming programs and to support those programs that were performing well. We survived the FBIHQ inspection I encountered upon my arrival, and we actually did alright after we updated the Buffalo program interrogatories to properly present the quality and depth of the work that the field office was performing.

We made some line supervisory changes and personnel updates over time, and most of the line supervisors would come to understand, accept, and execute my intent and performance expectations. One of the most important changes closest to me was the introduction of a new administrative specialist position to serve as the new SAC secretary. This role was highly sought after as it paid well and that person would determine who could see the SAC, wield the SAC's power, and would often serve as a top-echelon source of information for people around the office (which was often not a good thing for the SAC).

I was looking for a different role with updated skill sets, so I had the position converted from a secretary to an administrative specialist so I could pay a bit more and possibly attract more people who would be willing to apply. I ended up selecting an external candidate, meaning someone from the FBI but not from the Buffalo office. This choice made me an instant villain because there was an "heiresses apparent" that I was supposed to pick for the job. This person who had been "waiting" was considered next in line in everyone's eyes.

During the selection process for the new SAC "Secretary", I had the AO conduct interviews with all of the candidates to screen down to the top three. Then I joined the second round of interviews. In the end, the AO and I selected someone from FBIHQ who ended up being outstanding. My new administrative specialist (as the SAC Secretary) was exceptionally capable—she knew how to do almost anything I needed, and if she did not know something immediately, she figured it out quickly on her own. She solved problems and was an exceptional gatekeeper and protector of confidence. She was smart and trustworthy and had no prior social or familial entanglements in the office—gone was the top-echelon informant for activities in the SAC's office. She took care of all of the SAC's business and was unflappable in running the office. She allowed no people to congregate at her desk (which was an irritating legacy practice) and kept my business secure.

This exercise showed me that there must be a balance between bringing in new staff members and promoting those who have been waiting patiently for career enhancement opportunities. This balancing point must be weighed carefully against the organization's mission needs—and not assessed solely on personal relationships or whether the selection of an outside candidate might be unpopular. These tough decisions are fairly simple but may not be easy—just as with many leadership decisions.

Over time, most of the Buffalo supervisors rose to the occasion and began operating as capable professional FBI leaders—I really would not accept anything else as what we did was too important for the American people. The supervisors came up with good ideas and started looking past the easiest ways of complying with requirements. We implemented a series of weekly staff meetings, program reviews, budget and resource assessments, and business health and welfare checks that significantly improved program discipline and execution. These interactions also improved managerial engagement, as they now had to prepare for regular meetings with me.

In the beginning, the program briefs were slow, clunky, and of low value. After several rounds of these sessions and some instruction and coaching, the briefs became sharper, more focused, and more informative. I was encouraged by how the supervisors improved their overall program awareness and their articulation of operational activities. The changes were significant, and the Buffalo Field Office was beginning to perform at desired performance levels.

It was a long road, but the Buffalo Field Office steadily improved. Buffalo became a regular fixture in the five to ten top-performing field offices out of fifty-six across the US with regard to FBIHQ business health measures and investigative achievement. The office was looking good with a number of facility upgrades, and operations were moving closer to a new sustainable standard. Office professionalism had improved significantly across all programs, which was evident in the squad work products and the interactions I had with the staff.

During this tour of duty, I learned a lot about how to develop people and programs through mentoring, instruction, and direction for desired outcomes. I worked with the office leaders to consider the welfare of the organization and the mission and that of our personnel when making decisions. As a result, people began moving with a sense of purpose, we were getting things done, and office business was steadily improving.

Then, one day, I received a call from the deputy director. He told me to pack my things and get ready to come back to FBIHQ—the TSC director (identified earlier as Harrier) had put in his retirement notice and had recommended me as his successor. I was going back to the TSC, but this time I would be serving as the center director. While I thanked the deputy director for the opportunity, I quietly hoped that I would be worthy of the TSC mission, the staff, and Harrier's previous instruction. The role carried a heavy responsibility for twenty-four-hour worldwide counterterrorism watchlisting, screening, and threat detection. While I enjoyed my time in Buffalo, I was looking forward to getting back to the TSC. It was go-time.

FILE REVIEW

My time in Buffalo validated much of the leadership and management training and experience that I received up to that point—especially from my preceding tour of duty at the TSC. I took all of the knowledge from colleagues, mentors, and superiors and created my own operational model for how to run the Buffalo office. I saw my SAC tour of duty as an in-depth leadership exercise. The squad personnel were fairly static during my time in Buffalo, but the operational standards and expectations were changed significantly. As a leadership team, we formed common operating perspectives, clear expected outcomes, and a more defined leadership model. We improved the office's general business approach and set higher expectations for investigative performance and general professionalism. I saw clearly that instituting the proper leadership climate and practices was an effective way to motivate a mediocre organization to reform itself, set and sustain new standards, and perform well. I saw the power of focused, active leadership as a primary factor in determining whether an organization succeeds or fails. One last thought from General Bruce C. Clark (USA, Retired): "An organization does well only those things the boss checks." I saw this concept work firsthand. I checked things, and the Buffalo Field Office did well. There is no substitute for consistent, effective leadership.

" My assignment as the TSC director provided me with an opportunity to assemble a remarkable interagency team of senior leaders and program managers that worked tirelessly to keep people, places, and things safe around the world. "

12

DIRECTOR, TERRORIST SCREENING CENTER

I reported back to the TSC in April 2013 and assumed the role of center director. I was a bit concerned about the big shoes I had to fill. I was now an FBI assistant director, and the recently retired TSC director (Harrier) had been a fixture there for many years and had led the center to many successes and achievements. When I walked into the center, it did not appear that much had changed in an organizational sense since I was assigned there as the DD-Ops. As usual, I was wrong.

Directing the TSC

I met with the center's senior leaders and thanked them for keeping the place going while I was transitioning out of the Buffalo Field Office. I said that I looked forward to working with them in moving the center forward. After these initial discussions, I began noticing that the center's operating environment had indeed changed while I was gone. I saw that some of the center's leaders were not fully integrated in their work. In addition, conflicts had developed between some TSC leaders who were detailed to the center from the FBI and the DHS. After meeting with some of the center's external federal, state, and local partners, I was advised that the TSC had drifted to more of an inward-looking mode of operation. The relationship that appeared to atrophy the most was with the TSC's closest counterpart organization, the National Counterterrorism Center (NCTC). Like the TSC, the NCTC was also a multi-agency organization designed to receive and analyze intelligence to support global US counterterrorism efforts. I knew it would take some work to repair some of the key relationships that enabled the TSC's mission success, so I went to work. I began to visit my interagency partners at their places of business whenever possible to introduce myself as the new TSC director. I did a lot of listening and not a lot of talking as I took in the evolving concerns, needs, and interests of my partners. In many instances, the partners were just glad that I came to their office and listened to their thoughts.

After meeting with my key leadership staff and some of my operational partners, my next course of action was to recruit an exceptional person to become my special assistant. This person, MAC, would help me in managing the numerous lines of operation and business maintained by the TSC. MAC (who later served as my TSC chief of staff) was instrumental in keeping center operations aligned with our newly updated operational objectives. She was personally responsible for keeping everything moving while I went to meetings at FBIHQ or other government offices. In addition to being my conscience, protector, and reality anchor, MAC was also responsible for resolving routine center issues, maintaining project timelines, receiving program deliverables, doing quality control, checking operational alignment, and managing whatever emergent challenges arose on a daily basis. We decided that MAC needed some dedicated help, so we established a new administrative role, and she selected an outstanding management and program analyst to fill this role. This immediate staff change was essential to the efficient operation of the center's executive functions and administrative performance. With these two fantastic people working closely together in a Batman and Robin fashion, we hit new levels of efficiency for internal and external program management and coordination. The TSC began meeting deadlines and reporting requirements (which had become inconsistent and problematic). Active tracking of program milestones and submitting work progress reports became the norm. MAC's hard work and close coordination with me and the rest of the leadership team were essential in recalibrating and sustaining the TSC's updated practices to meet our new operational requirements. MAC was an outstanding business partner and friend, and I cannot thank her enough for her support and strong business sense that made the TSC a better place to be.

After becoming reacquainted with TSC's global watchlisting programs and receiving customer and partner feedback, I worked closely with the center's executive leaders to restructure our strategic plan, sharpen the center's interagency focus, and revamp the customer service approach. As part of this restructuring, I met with my federal agency counterparts—all senior government officials—and began working on some of the more strained relationships. I held friendly but focused conversations where we clarified common objectives; found mutual interests; and collaboratively designed, built, and maintained state-of-the-art national security watchlisting systems. After a series of discussions, in which I again listened more than I talked, I was able to advance collaboration while we resolved or minimized some of the prominent friction points. One of my primary courses of action was the establishment of a new Interagency Watchlisting Advisory Council, where I shared authority with my NCTC counterpart, and we served as co-chairs. We worked closely with our interagency partners, and we integrated technical systems, resources, and authorities to jointly develop global security policies for the National Security Council (NSC). Most of the partners just wanted to be heard and appreciated the chance to voice concerns and seek beneficial outcomes. These efforts received high praise from the NSC for resolving past friction and various challenges on our own and not needing any "adult supervision" to move forward.

While I was making strides with my interagency partners, I also began recalibrating my leadership approach as the director of the center. I made adjustments in how I managed center operations to accommodate being the head of a group of interagency SES-level leaders. I was now a strategic leader of strategic leaders and took input and advice from my teammates as means of guiding outcomes. I began to understand the difference more clearly between leading through command and control versus using instruction and influence to meet goals and objectives. I also became much more comfortable with a "leadership by intent" approach, where I provided my senior managers with expected outcomes and intended courses of action rather than stiff, prescriptive directions. The senior managers would then form their own plans of action with their staff members to meet my intent, which increased their personal ownership and enhanced overall center success.

Unfortunately, not everyone at the TSC was supportive of the changes we were making. Some TSC staff members wanted to maintain the status quo and were not supportive of the operating models and expectations that we were adopting. I let them know that we wanted them to stay and help us to advance and fulfill the TSC's global protective mission; however, we would not accept disruptive, undermining, or otherwise unproductive behaviors. We (the TSC senior leadership team) were honest and consistent in our messaging and actions, which were focused primarily on center mission achievement and NOT the personal interests or benefits of any person, program, or center partner. In some instances, we helped people find other professional opportunities that were more suited to their personal values and beliefs. In the end, some folks left the center, and some were disinvited from the center. It was nothing personal, but the TSC mission was more important than any of us, and we made sure that the staff clearly understood that.

After a year or so of making program updates, strengthening partnerships, and reorienting our staff to the center's new operating principles and expectations, we saw operations level out and then improve notably. The center's senior program managers and staff members were moving things forward, and the TSC was performing as the premier counterterrorism organization that the world needed it to be.

A Broader View

As a US government interagency enterprise service provider, the TSC required a global view that took into account more than just the FBI's mission. I now oversaw a responsibility set that covered the needs of federal, state, local, tribal, and territorial law enforcement; intelligence organizations; national fusion centers; international diplomatic initiatives; military operations, transportation safety; border point of entry screening, immigration processing; and maritime security. As I learned earlier in my career, I was personally responsible for covering the FBI's interests. Now I was also now personally responsible for the welfare of all of my constituent partners and customers that comprised the global screening system. I would need a worldview and a strong team of partners to meet emerging threat environments and yet-to-be-identified challenges based on what was the emerging phenomenon of foreign fighters being drawn to conflict regions in the Middle East.

A new group was forming, the Islamic State of Iraq and Syria (ISIS), that would soon take the centerpiece in the world of counterterrorism conversations and operations. The TSC and its partners would be challenged with the movement of global fighters moving around the world to support ISIS. The US and its national security partners did not have the ability to capture or eliminate all potential fighters, but the TSC could do its part and manage and interdict their movements, identify logistical channels, and recognize the new types of tradecraft being developed to evade our surveillance and security networks. These activities required a global network to protect national interests. The TSC and its partners were the silent backbone of this network.

In this respect, I served a group of international security partners to provide twenty-four-hour monitoring and interdiction of terrorism and transnational organized crime activities. Now, I had to manage our expansion of mission scope more strategically. So, I worked with my TSC leadership team and partners in developing enterprise perspectives that built and enhanced layered security infrastructures outside of FBI operations and authorities. As I was regularly attending meetings at the NSC to develop and steer certain counterterrorism policies and practices, one instance brought all of these activities together in our worldwide terrorism interdiction mission.

In support of the TSC's global interagency mission, I became one of the primary negotiators for international security arrangements on behalf of the US government for Homeland Security Presidential Directive Six. Under this program, I worked with my governmental partners, traveled to various countries, and negotiated joint security partnerships that expanded our ability to detect and prevent acts of terrorism and serious crime. In one situation, I had to pool my skills and experiences to resolve a problem that had White House-level attention. It was a complicated situation, but I will summarize it here.

An international partner had repeatedly rejected US government overtures to formalize a counterterrorism security arrangement. Efforts were made by the State Department, the NSC, and other diplomatic connections, but none were successful. The threat of a formal démarche was made. A "name and shame" approach was entertained. Yet the partner would not acquiesce. Finally, I asked for the opportunity to meet with them. When we arrived, the head of the international partner agency greeted us. I introduced myself and thanked the agency head for his time. He smiled and said, "They finally let the policeman speak." We both laughed, and then we talked about the challenges of global counterterrorism operations. At no time did I ask him to do anything, nor did I allude to any kind of agreement. I listened to his concerns, and then I was able to read between the lines. Basically, he did not possess the technical capabilities required to do what was being asked by the US. There it was. The US government merely assumed that the partner had the capability but never asked. I saw the opening. I thanked the partner for his hospitality, and then I made a proposal. I offered to build a secure Internet-based portal where the partner agency could upload its counterterrorism screening data. I advised that my staff take the data, run searches against the TSC's watchlisting holdings, and return a report that the agency could use to sharpen its operations (and possibly save the partner some time and money). All the agency head had to do was complete our security agreement and then receive the service. He was amazed that we could do that, and he agreed to sign the agreement. We completed the agreement, and the exceptional TSC IT unit chief and his team built the required IT systems in about sixty days. We then began accepting the partner's screening submissions. This was a great success for the US government and the TSC. As a result of my ability to keep my mouth shut, be patient (not my greatest strength), and not force a solution, we came to an amicable resolution of a long-standing problem with a valued international partner. We provided a way for the partner to save face, and we used our considerable technical capability to deliver a new counterterrorism service that would later become a standard offering for other less capable global security partners. Bottom line: We closed a major counterterrorism screening gap and expanded our new portal as a service for other partners who lacked the technical resources to identify threats. The NSC was surprised and thankful that we could get this done with local resources and without the usual requests for more funding and manpower.

National-Level Issues, Great People, and Moving On

During this time, I learned how to work under national leaders by providing policy support and testimony to congressional committees and members. I had the privilege of overseeing the operation of the US government's terror watchlist, and I served as the chief adjudicator for the "no fly" list, which barred people from accessing United States air travel without proper security measures and policy waivers. As such, I would receive regular inquiries from Capitol Hill about counterterrorism watchlisting policies, practices, and the real or perceived impact to US citizens. I was also summoned to the Hill for briefings on specific watchlisting situations. During these meetings, I learned that some of our national leaders were actually quite reasonable when cameras and the media were not present. I was fortunate to sit with congressional members and their staffs and explain the mechanics of the US counterterrorism watchlisting system. I answered their questions and tried my best to dispel the absolute silliness that dominated the Internet and the twenty-four-hour news cycle regarding the US counterterrorism watchlisting enterprise. We often left with good results.

In one instance, I was speaking with a room full of congressional members in what was coined an "informational brief." I was answering questions when one of the members asked, "Do you track members of the NRA on your watchlist?"

I said no.

Then the member said, "How can you be sure?"

I responded, "Ma'am, I am positive that we do not track NRA members because I am a member of the NRA."

She laughed along with the rest of the room and advised that she, too, was an NRA member.

That day, I was able to clarify many other misconceptions about the TSC's operations. As a result of our candor, professionalism, command of subject matter, and mission clarity, I believe we made a few friends that day. For these types of discussions, of which there were many, I have to give credit to my outstanding TSC legal team, which always helped me to see the proverbial "bigger picture" when we participated in national-level policy development, congressional discussions, and other sensitive business areas. The team worked tirelessly to avoid bear traps and keep the TSC and me out of trouble in many instances when just any kind of "free legal advice" would never be good enough.

My assignment as the TSC director provided me with an opportunity to assemble a remarkable interagency team of senior leaders and program managers that worked tirelessly to keep people, places, and things safe around the world. In this group of exceptional people, I had the chance to work closely with some of the smartest, wisest people I had met in my career. These leaders never let the TSC, the American people, or me down. I was privileged to work with a cadre of superior information technology professionals who were led by an outstanding program unit chief. This person helped me to oversee one of the largest information technology programs maintained by the FBI, where we processed approximately ten terabytes of identity information per day (which is certainly more now). As matter of context, the Hubble Space Telescope delivers approximately ten terabytes of data per year. I could go on about other remarkable people at the TSC, but there are too many to mention without making this book a TSC staff member tribute. It was because of the outstanding people at the TSC that I was given the opportunity grow and mature as a senior government official and not just an FBI executive leader. I learned a lot about being a C-level executive, and I decided that I would likely remain at the TSC as the center director until my retirement from federal service.

I had just passed three years in the TSC director role, and I was still enjoying the center because it was a great place to work. We were doing outstanding work in supporting the US government's global security mission. The center's mission was essential, and the staff members were still, by and large, outstanding. All was good in my world—for a bit.

Then one morning, one of our TSC executive staff members came into my office and said that the FBI director was on the phone. I laughed and said, "Okay." She assured me that she was not kidding. I answered the phone, greeted the director, and asked how I could be of assistance. He did not mince words, saying that he was going to change my world. I was not sure what that meant—if this was going to be really good or really bad. Maybe he was going to ask me to retire. He then said that he wanted me to be his next executive assistant director (EAD) for the FBI's Science and

Director, Terrorist Screening Center

Technology Branch (STB). The departing EAD-STB had requested a return to field operational duty as an SAC. I was a bit speechless. Being an EAD meant that I would become one of the six strategic managers who provided oversight for the six primary FBI program branches. I would become one of the most senior FBI SES managers and report directly to the FBI deputy director. This was a more advanced C-level role that would be the rough equivalent of a chief operations officer, chief technology officer, or chief executive officer of a medium-sized business. I snapped out of my stupor and told the director that I would be honored and that I was flattered by his consideration. He said, "Good," and then he told me to coordinate a transition plan with the deputy director. Then he hung up, and I sat there for a minute.

I felt a bit sick about leaving the TSC, its mission, and its people. I would be moving back to main FBIHQ to lead the FBI's largest program branch (the Science and Technology Branch) with the most assigned personnel and the largest operating budget. This was unexpected, and I hoped it would be the right way to complete my career.

FILE REVIEW

The main point in this file review is that I worked among a group of dedicated, highly capable people. They professionally safeguarded the safety and security of the American public, as well as everyone around the world who could be subjected to the scourge of terrorism. My time at the TSC will always be one of my most treasured career experiences because I learned a lot about executive leadership and how to deal with people on all levels. It was because of their high caliber that I developed a better sense of when to manage and when to lead—which are not the same. We lead people, and we manage activities. People can do remarkable things and will work themselves practically to death, without being asked, if a few basic factors are present:

- They are provided with a mission or cause they believe in.
- They are given a principled operating environment where they feel heard, valued, and respected.
- They are provided with leaders they can consistently depend on for honesty, objectivity, good judgment, and consideration for others.

Note: None of these factors cost money, but they can mean everything to organizational success.

“I saw many of the usual bureaucratic stalling tactics and parades of excuses popping up like an anti-aircraft artillery defense network. We had a lot of work to do.”

13

FBIHQ EXECUTIVE ASSISTANT DIRECTOR—SCIENCE AND TECHNOLOGY BRANCH

I reported for duty as the FBI's new EAD-STB at the end of October 2016. I talked with the director and deputy director about their expectations, and I wrote a list of their respective general areas of interest and their combined areas of concern. After creating action plans to address these areas, I talked with my fellow EADs (as well as my predecessor, the outgoing EAD-STB) to determine how they viewed the services and products provided by the STB. I was well acquainted with the other sitting EADs, and we formed a collegial atmosphere that focused on how we could best support each other and advance the FBI mission. That meant that they felt no need for pleasantries and quickly gave me some candid feedback. Basically, some of them did not feel that STB was adequately supporting their operational priorities and needs. I appreciated my fellow EADs' candor, as it was our responsibility to work together and ensure that the priority FBI operational programs were as effective and efficient as possible.

Assessing Areas for Improvement— Another Cycle of Change

I was directly advised by the deputy director and some of the other EADs that some STB components might have become overly focused on their own operations and became distracted from the greater customer service mission. Another area for attention was that the STB major components did not work together in integrating their respective resources and capabilities under a unified set of strategic branch initiatives. The STB components—the Operational Technology Division (OTD), the Laboratory Division (Lab), and the Criminal Justice Information Services Division (CJIS)—were national asset programs that provided specialized technological and science-based products and services for the law enforcement, national security, and cyber missions of the FBI and its partners. Yet, these divisions were all happy doing their own thing and were not necessarily interested in a unified approach to conducting business.

At the time, the STB worked with a multi-billion-dollar operating budget and a geographically dispersed staff of about 5,500, so the branch's operations had the ability to impact a host of FBI enterprise program outcomes. As such, I began meeting with the assistant directors (ADs) who ran the three STB divisions. We talked about the prevailing operational and business models of their respective organizations. I asked them to review their strategic plans and their program goals and objectives to assess how well they were supporting our customers and partners—because I would be doing the same.

Based on the feedback I received from my now-fellow EADs and some field office SACs, I urged the STB ADs to look at their primary projects and initiatives and determine how well we, as a branch, were supporting the FBI's corporate programmatic priorities. After these discussions, I provided the entire branch with an email that outlined my expectations. Some things were about change.

People, Programs, and Systems

I worked with the STB executive staff to learn about the branch operations in such areas as budgeting, strategy, performance measurement, and program management. As this assessment moved forward, I split my analysis into three areas: people, programs, and systems.

- For people, we took a broad view of our human capital to determine if we had personnel gaps and if we had the right people with the right attributes in the right roles. We also looked at each division to determine if we had the required leadership culture on all levels.
- For programs, we reviewed our mission to assess alignment with FBI enterprise objectives. We also evaluated continued relevance and benefit. We talked with program managers to reform strategies to promote improved organizational alignment and integration in terms of how STB assets were supporting the broader FBI mission set.
- For systems, our reviews spanned across the STB divisions—technical, logistical, and administrative—that were in place to operate key STB infrastructures that sustained complex investigative and technological efforts. We also worked with division managers to verify the stability and security of STB information technology systems.

We found instances in which STB and its constituent divisions had allowed mediocrity, irrelevance, and bureaucratic indifference to seep into our operating model. This seepage was not the fault of any one person or program. It was due to an accumulation of time, extended personnel tenures in certain programs, some personality-based operations, and the high-tech approach of baffling higher levels of leadership with technological bullshit. Of course, we, at STB, had to cut through the bullshit and prioritize certain issues for immediate attention, and the divisions did their thing and tried to find ways to avoid scrutiny and fight to retain as much status quo as possible.

Being a technology-based organization, I organized STB program discussions into three main areas to help everyone understand what we were doing and how we used the FBI's technological and scientific resources:

- **Operational Technology:** This area was mainly the purview of the OTD, which provided the FBI and its partners with the James Bond–like tools for agents to engage the threat environment for surveillance, clandestine data collection, offensive cyber operations, secure communications, and other sensitive activities. We used technology to help case agents and their counterpart intelligence analysts to engage and defeat a multitude of threat issues.
- **Infrastructure Technology:** This area was shared by all three of the STB divisions (OTD, Lab, and CJIS). The STB provided information technology to support asset communications, scientific applications, and criminal justice data management for the entire country. It also provided enterprise services to the law enforcement and intelligence communities that advanced lawful security activities and also protected civil liberties and privacy.

- **Enabling Technology:** This area provided users with automation, digitization, and analytical capabilities that made FBI investigative efforts more efficient and economical. Improved information collection/management and automation were large parts of this area. STB's primary objective was to provide technical solutions to enhance the effectiveness of FBI case agents and their counterpart intelligence analysts to quickly detect, assess, and deter national security threats and criminal activities.

When I began asking in-depth questions of the division managers about their business models and leadership approaches, I frequently received less-than-enthusiastic responses. I heard a lot of smokescreen feedback and evasive nonsense from program managers on several levels. I knew I was invading some well-established fiefdoms that had taken hold over the years across all divisions. I saw many of the usual bureaucratic stalling tactics and parades of excuses popping up like an anti-aircraft artillery defense network. We had a lot of work to do.

As we looked more closely at STB operations, we ran into a host of personality-driven operations that were more like hobby shops than sharply focused FBI investigative programs (similar to my program experiences in Buffalo). When we asked about certain practices and outcomes, we were repeatedly met with a mix of defensive attitudes and program parochialism. I clearly saw how many of the STB program managers had adopted the "resist and justify" approach where they accepted no external feedback, resisted any questioning of their practices, and blindly justified what they are doing. All of this despite instances where we saw a lack of results, an absence of a good business model, or the inability to articulate reasonable alignment with FBI or STB expectations. I also saw that some of the STB program managers had been in their roles too long or possibly should not have been there at all given the mission requirements. I knew we had our work cut out for us in motivating the divisions to begin professionalizing their leadership approaches, driving ownership and accountability with their staff members, and modernizing their business models. So, we went to work.

Implementing Change, Yet Again

I began implementing strategic shifts that required movements away from inward-looking program practices to outward-looking customer service models. I also started initiating some cultural changes to return the STB to a higher level of customer service. I required that the divisions begin working more closely with their customers and partners to see what was needed and whether some customer needs were not being addressed. We were no longer going to operate for the sake of our own operations. I discovered that our partners had been forming their own technical subprograms to meet their own needs. This was completely unsatisfactory and was a giant warning that STB had not been providing the services and products that were needed or wanted in a timely fashion, if at all.

To begin driving toward our updated STB focus areas, I included preferred business practices in the SES performance appraisals of the assistant directors who led the subordinate STB divisions. These practices were formulated to promote collaboration among the STB's divisions to meet newly formed branch-level objectives. The SES performance appraisal was the baseline assessment tool to rate FBI executive performance and served as a major influence in encouraging preferred behaviors. These appraisals were also used to determine any monetary bonuses that could be awarded at the end of the yearly performance period, so SES-level managers were often motivated to be successful in fulfilling their objectives.

I began visiting all of the STB divisions to discuss and reinforce my cultural and business expectations. I developed periodic email messages that provided instruction (and periodic reinforcement) on how the branch and its divisions would be expected to conduct business internally as well as externally with customers and partners. I also required new visibility into each division's operations. I instructed STB executive staff program managers to coordinate budgeting, strategy, and information management activities to promote consistency and collaboration between the STB other FBIHQ entities. Working with my STB executive staff, we issued updated branch-level focus areas. I worked with the assistant directors of the STB divisions to provide resources and support to advance the FBI's corporate capabilities in the areas of information technology, biometrics, business efficiency, and technological and scientific development. These updated focus areas promoted joint initiatives and collaborations among the STB divisions to help meet these expectations.

It is worth noting that the STB executive staff had been previously seen primarily as a tasking function that the divisions did not really appreciate (as the division heads enthusiastically told me). After a recalibration, the STB executive staff would begin serving as more of a resource to the divisions and would provide support and coordination for branch-level program management operations. This support would include finance, strategic planning, communications, legal review, policy development, compliance, project management, and inter-branch coordination.

I must recognize the efforts of two key people on the STB executive staff. First, my chief of staff from the TSC, MAC, was kind enough to transfer with me to the STB and help me get set up. She was always a good soldier and continued to serve as my protector, conscience, business partner, and valued colleague. However, after some time, the long commute to FBIHQ from her residence was wearing on her, so I secured another position that would improve her quality of life (but certainly not mine). I was sad to see her go, but I asked her to help me find a replacement as she was familiar with my work habits and idiosyncrasies. She recommended another TSC member who recently transferred to the STB executive staff. This person, Anna, would be my business manager for the rest of my STB tour of duty. She would be my new protector and conscience. She would coordinate activities and monitor branch functions while I attended endless rounds of meetings. Anna was also a strategy wizard, so she helped refine our STB strategic plans. I could not have gotten STB business where it had to be without Anna. She spent more time in the seventh-floor "blast zone" than most anyone else and became an outstanding partner, trusted colleague, and friend.

Communication with the STB divisions could be a bit sticky in a few areas, but it all began to smooth out, and some good working relationships were taking hold. All it took was excellent program management from the executive staff, leadership backing from the division heads, and the establishment of common operating perspectives to break down many of the fiefdoms. We still had work to do, and we began looking at changes to our leadership teams and our operating approaches.

The Value of New Leaders

I eventually selected new ADs for the STB divisions as the incumbents retired. Fortunately, I was able to select new senior executive leaders for their leadership capabilities and attributes. These new leaders, as AD-level division heads, were also willing to change some of the less-than-outstanding status quo approaches that were still alive and well in the divisions—but might have gone underground to avoid corrective attention.

I did not always follow the usual FBI practice of taking the most senior (tenured), the most popular, or the most technically skilled person for the job. We had a lot of very smart candidates, but I felt that we needed true organizational leaders at the AD level to advance. We did not necessarily need the smartest people to be in charge of other highly credentialed scientists or technologists nor were we running a popularity contest. My new executive leaders were energetic, highly capable, and willing to move forward under my vision and our updated STB business perspectives and models. Things were beginning to look up.

The branch was becoming more structured in its practices and was more effective in its program management and the delivery of program results for our customers and partners. STB strategic alignment was now clear and coherent and could be tied to a unified set of objectives (thanks to my business manager, Anna and the new STB Chief of Staff). Our collaboration with internal and external customers and partners continued to improve. I was beginning to receive more positive feedback than complaints from customers and partners, which was a good sign.

STB personnel were now deploying with FBI investigators for field operations and crisis responses, and we were once again being sought out by the bureau's operational divisions as valued mission partners. We were supporting our US intelligence community colleagues as well as our international partners. I was happy with the overall progress being made throughout the branch. We were seeing new levels of leadership effectiveness, program discipline, and operational success. We still had some work to do but I saw that true organizational development and performance improvement were possible within government channels with the right leadership culture, assertive strategic alignment, and engaged executive program management. All was pretty good.

FILE REVIEW

Effective, measured leadership was the most important factor that enabled everything else. Because of it, we were able to develop common operating perspectives and sustain the program results that were necessary for FBI success. We took this approach and ferreted out several organizational challenges, which was painful, but had to be done.

In one instance, The AD-OTD and I had to deliver bad news to Director Wray about a controversial program and its statistical data that had been shared with the public and with FBI detractors. We found a programming error that artificially inflated certain statistics, thereby creating historical errors in select cyber-related FBI reporting. It was the closest that I had seen Director Wray to being visibly angry. He was disgusted and told us to get it fixed.

While the data management error occurred before the presiding AD-OTD and I were in our positions, we owned the error. We took the heat with the director and made the necessary corrections in how applicable data sets were being collected and processed. It was embarrassing and painful, but we would not hide behind weak excuses or blame-shifting. We did not do business that way. The programming may not have been done properly under previous conditions, but we had to put everything right, even at our own professional expense. It took leadership and some thick skin on many levels to recover—but recover we did, albeit with some egg on our faces. Principled leadership and ownership make things right and keep things right. That is it.

" When I see media reports and footage, I am often confused by the state of what my FBI has become, what its priorities and practices have evolved into, and how it now conducts its business. "

14

MOVING TOWARD THE LAST MILE

While I was happy with the evolving state of STB business, working at the EAD level could be demanding and exhausting. It could also be corrosive to personal well-being at times. One of the primary reasons for this corrosiveness was the emergence of a different leadership environment after Director Comey departed. In addition to Comey's departure, the sitting deputy director and acting FBI director, Andrew McCabe, was subsequently removed after unproductive interactions with the White House. After these inglorious transitions, the FBI received a new director, Christopher Wray, and a new deputy director and a new associate deputy director were selected.

Director Wray brought in some of his own staff members and the leadership climate changed at the top levels of the FBI, causing the beginning of what I saw as a downward trend. The optimism and lighter atmosphere that were favored by former Director Comey, for better or worse, started to dissipate. Director Wray was getting his bearings and was quickly being isolated by his own staff—and possibly by his own preference. Director Wray was a decent person (as far as I could tell), but he was standoffish in his general demeanor and did not seem as approachable as former Director Comey.

Director Wray was more arms-length in his interactions with his senior leadership team, which further chilled the climate on the famed (or infamous) "Seventh Floor" where most of the senior FBI leaders resided at the J. Edgar Hoover Building in Washington, DC.

While we continued to meet each morning to brief Director Wray on bureau business and global operational developments, the tone of the meetings became mechanical, and the discussions felt stifled. These meetings were losing their benefit in building camaraderie and common operating perspectives among the FBI's senior leadership team. There was a lack of levity compared to the meetings with Director Comey. Smaller, closed, invitation-only meetings soon became the norm. After a meeting's initial briefing, most of the attendees would be curtly excused, and only certain people would remain to talk about "sensitive" issues. From my conversations with other senior leaders, this practice created a fractured feeling among the top echelon. I saw us heading toward an environment of information stovepipes, cliques, and insular communications that were part of an unfavorable direction for the FBI. Director Wray's personal staff was essentially worthless in working with the rest of the organization. Wray's staff members further insulated him from the EADs and other senior managers who should have been the director's primary protectors, but were slowly being pushed away from him. The deterioration continued with higher levels of FBI management becoming more interested in what sounded good versus what actually worked well.

The FBI was heading toward some tough times, but we did not see it coming yet. People were too busy focusing on close-range issues, personal agendas, and appearances, while the organization at large was still settling down after the recent abrupt changes in top leadership.

Retirement

The morning meetings with the director and deputy director became a chore over time. We no longer talked as a united bureau senior leadership team. Individuals became worried about their own pressing issues, and it became difficult to measure the organization's corporate health and welfare. The director and deputy director were no longer building teamwork and actively requiring mutually integrated operations among the branches and divisions. Sure, there was talk about teamwork, but we were not really practicing it in delivering results.

I sat and listened to my colleagues as they provided their program briefs in various meetings, but it was in the hallways and other informal settings that I gained insight into the challenges that the organization was starting to encounter. I began seeing inconsistencies in how the major programs worked together (or not)—they began to drift apart as people started seeking the deputy director's attention and favor. I saw leadership cliques and alliances form, and certain people and programs were receiving preferential attention from the director, deputy director, and associate deputy director. Instead of well-thought-out logical business and operational approaches, I began to see an increase in organizational decisions being fueled by personal agendas and turf battles. Objective data analyses, investigative rigor, beneficial program reviews, threat assessments, and good practices seemed to be secondary in practice and fading.

I was disappointed by the decisions made by executive fiat on the part of the deputy director. He began making more and more unilateral operational and administrative decisions that surprised many people. My colleagues in different parts of the organization would call me and ask, "What the hell is going on with the Seventh Floor?" These questions were frequently posed by SACs in the field or from senior or intermediate managers throughout the FBIHQ program structure.

I was also navigating emerging shadow management structures that were being formed by the executive staffs of the director, deputy director, and associate deputy director, as well as by some of the senior leadership cliques. Some executive staff members were helpful and tried to do the right things for the right reasons; however, many of them added significant complexity, and sometimes outright nonsense, to the management of various bureau operations. These often-unhelpful staff members began using the authority of their executive principals to advance their own personal preferences and had to be chastised when they tried to influence activities outside of their organizational stations. Centralized decision-making was becoming the norm with the deputy director and associate deputy director, which I believed was a sign that the organization was struggling or in distress.

The FBI's relocation of programs and personnel to the Redstone Arsenal in Huntsville, Alabama, was one such issue. The deputy and associate deputy directors began these relocations through the FBI's often-maligned Resource Planning Office (RPO). The RPO was a holdover from the SET days when the bureau hired a group of people from the SET consultant environment and formed its own internal consultant group. With regard to the Huntsville project, the RPO began tasking the EADs and ADs to move people and programs to Redstone Arsenal. Unfortunately, the RPO failed to understand that moving certain programs away from the national capital region would have dire negative effects on the FBI's operational capabilities; however, the RPO began making its own plans on behalf of the deputy and associate deputy directors. The EADs were given the illusion of input and choice, but many decisions had already been made. Additional worthless meetings just became forums to socialize these decisions.

In one of these worthless meetings on the Huntsville matter, I asked the associate deputy director to simply give the order and we would execute his wishes. He advised that he did not want to do that, probably out of fear of getting negative feedback from the workforce (which seemed to be a primary concern for him). To be fair, there was certainly value in relocating specific FBI operations to Huntsville, but the people making recommendations and decisions on what should move did not have the proper program insights to make such judgments. This was quickly becoming the way things were managed from the top through non-agent managers in the RPO. The Huntsville matter outlasted me and was still in progress when I departed government service. I can only hope that some common sense was added to the discussions to preserve FBI operational capabilities.

In other bureau business matters, the deputy director began inserting himself into a number of lower-level matters that normally would have been dealt with by intermediate managers. He also started ignoring the established chains of command and began contacting people directly, which caused varying levels of chaos and disarray across affected programs. He started making decisions without informing his senior leadership team, and we had to resolve the consequences. This lack of discipline in the chain of command made the FBIHQ senior leadership cadre look less coordinated, less capable, and sometimes ridiculous to staff members. Discipline and order began to quietly suffer but this was just the beginning.

The deputy director gradually stopped communicating effectively with senior leaders but put great effort into being liked by junior personnel. The deputy director was a likable person overall, and I believe he meant well, but his role was not to be the hero who gave people what they wanted at the expense of operational discipline, crisp mission execution, and unified leadership for the organization. He drifted into full savior mode, and I feel that he tried to fix things, but he was really not helping anything. The deputy director even went as far as telling people that he had CHSs who were giving him information about what was happening in various parts of the organization. "CHS" stands for Confidential Human Source, or simply an informant. What were we supposed to think about the deputy director using informants (in his own words) to burrow into things far below his organizational attention level? What I can tell you is that he was not addressing larger, more strategic issues that were eroding organizational performance and pushing the bureau away from its roots.

I did not always agree with certain decisions and courses of action coming from above me, but I always tried to be honest and positive in passing direction to other organizational levels that I oversaw. I did not complain much—at least I tried not to. I just found myself solving the self-inflicted problems that would follow and providing explanations to employees as positively and honestly as I could. In the end, I would execute the wishes of my superiors as if they were my own (as much as I could) to protect my superiors (as much as I could) while also promoting FBI professionalism. I felt that I was fighting a losing battle.

I grew increasingly disgusted with the new office politics and the declining leadership environment, but I found extreme fault with the new FBI leadership trend that focused on being popular and getting good climate survey scores. Too much interest was placed on conducting business like private-sector corporate organizations instead of reinforcing the values and practices that made the FBI effective. The bureau was drifting further away from its roots and its mission-focused discipline, but the leadership favored an approach of coddling people and tolerating non-performance to keep the peace and minimize complaints.

In addition, the new FBI leadership environment seemed to favor people who had the ear of the deputy director or associate deputy director. The director, deputy director, and associate deputy director began to listen only to each other and to a few people who told them what they wanted to hear. They allowed certain individuals to gain undue influence in areas outside of their program oversight with little discernable rhyme or reason. Some senior FBI leadership selections were made to suit the deputy director's preferences and not necessarily what the organization required to promote excellence and maintain discipline. I saw several instances of senior leaders being selected for jobs (or not) based on their relationships, popularity, or other attributes that had little to do with their qualifications. Certain personnel exceptions and contrived circumstances were made by the deputy director for people he personally placed into senior leader positions. As mentioned earlier, the deputy director was in full savior mode and was determined to fix all of the organization's problems himself. Despite the deputy director's best efforts. we were starting to move into an organizational death spiral in how and where the FBI was being led.

All of this was occurring while the director seemed to drift further out of touch with workplace issues. The deputy director continued on a path of unilateral decision-making and managing program activities at far lower organizational levels than warranted his attention. I began to think that these lower levels of decision-making might have been where he was more comfortable. Who can tell? The associate deputy director was of little assistance other than to deliver bad news, provide negative feedback, or complain about chickenshit issues that had little bearing on how well the FBI was performing. It should be noted that the associate deputy director was eventually promoted into the deputy director role and holds that position as of the writing of this book. This operational and managerial environment was becoming detrimental for the FBI. Many of the actions taken during this time would plant the seeds for some of the challenges the FBI would encounter or create for itself over the next several years. I wished I still had some of the old breed special agents around to deliver honest critiques and help set things right, but they were all but gone. Most had retired and were watching from the civilian world and wondering what the hell was going on with their FBI. I would soon find myself doing the same.

Time to Do Something Else

I felt like the proverbial dinosaur and that I was out of place in the iteration of the FBI that had taken hold in the 2018-2019 timeframe. Many of my fellow EADs had retired, and I was the last person left from the collegial group I originally joined in 2016. When I looked around, I saw that this was no longer the FBI I joined nearly twenty-five years before. I know that times change but I no longer felt that I belonged in what the bureau had become (or was becoming). The values of the now-departed senior agents from my early career were largely discarded and replaced with more "modern" leadership practices characterized by exceedingly lax maintenance of organizational standards and lowered performance expectations.

I watched my FBI go from an organization with pride to being a prideful organization. Egos and turf battles had taken priority over mission focus and good business. It was time for me to do something else.

Every retired special agent I had previously spoken with told me that I would know when it was time to retire. They were right. At the end of January 2020, I retired from the FBI after nearly twenty-five years of service. I had a fantastic career, and I could not have asked for a better way to spend that quarter of a century of my life. I met some of the most fantastic people in the world. I worked with outstanding colleagues. I was blessed with exceptional staff members. I made a few lifetime friends. I worked for some exemplary leaders who taught me how to lead, how to treat people, and how to manage the no-fail operations for the legendary organization the FBI used to be. I got to do amazing things around the world in support of the FBI mission. I also met people who showed me how NOT to do things, how NOT to behave, and how NOT to conduct business. These lessons were just as valuable. All said, I felt that I had played a meaningful role in protecting the American people and upholding the Constitution. I believed that I could look back, feel that my efforts were worthy, and know that I had contributed to the safety and security of our great nation and its people.

On my final day of FBI duty, I unwillingly participated in a small farewell gathering with my STB executive staff and a few close colleagues (This gathering was held against my wishes, but my outstanding branch business manager and STB executive staff no longer cared about my wishes at this point.), I opted out of the usual FBIHQ pomp and circumstance that most EADs participated in when they retired. As I left the FBI, I was not looking for any self-celebration, but my executive staff was determined to give me a small send-off and provide me with one last gesture of their kindness to remember them by. I would miss them all.

Neither the deputy director nor the associate deputy director, both of whom I had been acquainted with for years, had time to say farewell. This was disappointing but not surprising. It was just an example of what the FBI had become.

It was customary for any departing EAD to have an outgoing discussion with the FBI director. During what would be my last official visit with Director Wray, I told him I learned that, among the US government's many agencies and organizations, the FBI and uniformed US military were the two most trusted government institutions that the American people looked for and turned to during or after a crisis. I also said that the FBI's primary currencies were its credibility and competence earned through the accomplishment and sacrifice of previous FBI generations. These currencies characterized the FBI values that made the organization worthy of the public's trust. I said that the director was the primary protector and champion of the FBI brand and that I had begun to see a decline in some areas of that brand. The director listened politely but said little.

Before I finished this perfunctory conversation, I advised the director that his most pressing leadership concern would be the GS-15 grade organizational managers. In various instances, people occupying GS-15 positions around the FBI may have been prematurely or erroneously promoted into that most senior of the GS pay grades (the equivalent of the military's O-6 rank—a full bird colonel in the US Army). I had observed varying instances where some of these GS-15 managers were not properly setting FBI cultural examples or capable of executing operational policies and practices in line with prior performance expectations. I told him that his problems would not likely be with his SES managers or other senior leaders who were eager to please him and would obey and execute orders in line with their personal capabilities. The director told me that he had not heard this type of assessment before. I was not surprised, as he had become effectively isolated and was fed only good news, happy talk, and general bullshit that caused him to think that everything was going better than it really was. When I could tell that the meeting was over, I did not think he truly heard a word I said. He politely wished me well, and my last lackluster meeting with Director Wray was over.

Finality

I entered onto duty with the FBI in 1995 with zero fanfare but with the greatest sense of humility and appreciation to be part of the organization. I decided to depart in the same fashion. As I have been told by people of great wisdom, all good things must end. I left the FBI Headquarters building for the last time on January 31, 2020, with my wife giving me a quiet ride home. I have not been back since.

I continue to miss the mission, the people, and the sense of purpose that I felt over the course of my FBI career. When I see media reports and footage, I am often confused by the state of what my FBI has become, what its priorities and practices have evolved into, and how it now conducts its business. I am disappointed by the possible decline in effective leadership and the perceived erosion in the fidelity, bravery, and integrity of an organization that once set the standard in these areas. Despite some of its challenges and failings throughout its history, I still believe that the FBI was once one of the finest organizations to ever exist. It could be again with an immediate, aggressive return to the leadership, culture, and mission focus that made it legendary.

That said, I would still go back and do it all over again.

FILE REVIEW

This is my last file review. When an organization finds itself struggling and falling short on performance, the senior leadership must think long and hard about how much centralized control should be exerted and for how long. Extended centralized leadership can have long-term damaging effects on an organization's culture and morale. While centralized control may be necessary and even beneficial in managing a short-term crisis, such leadership should be short-lived and transitory. If the organization has wisely chosen its leaders and has built a professional, accountable, results-oriented culture, then such an organization can effectively respond to most any crisis, manage consequences, and quickly restore order. Bottom line: Let people do their jobs or get the right people to do the jobs.

I saw the power of how senior leaders set the tone for why and how things are done—for better or worse. Rather than becoming mired in low-level business matters, senior leaders should focus on instilling and modeling enduring values that will fuel organizational success. Failure to establish a principled culture, maintain standards, develop true leaders, and encourage success will eventually lead to the death of excellence in any organization. This may not necessarily mean that the organization ceases to exist. It simply limps along without resilience, enthusiasm, or effectiveness but continues to survive (especially in government channels).

The United States cannot allow the death of its FBI. I am not talking about its daily operations but about the death of the warrior spirit, the demise of public trust, and the cultural failure of the FBI that has been charged to be our protector from all enemies, foreign and domestic, since its inception. The FBI that once set the standard for the law enforcement profession through its excellence, objectivity, and professionalism. The FBI that is rapidly becoming the proverbial "Last of the Mohicans."

File closed.

SECTION II

THE DECLINE OF THE FBI: WHAT WENT WRONG?

"I am still holding on to what the FBI was to me and what it could be again."

15

FIDELITY, BRAVERY, AND INTEGRITY—WHAT HAPPENED?

Since my departure in 2020, I have watched the FBI weather a number of storms and become entangled in various controversies and tight spots. Some of these situations could have been caused by misreading the operating environment or social sentiment. It happens. Maybe the FBI had not been as astute in navigating the highly partisan political landscape? Some problems could have been self-inflicted, as a result of distracted leadership or some organizational blind spots. Possibly, the FBI had experienced an erosion in its commitment to maintaining a strong sense of accountability and service to the American people. It is hard to tell exactly what happened because the bureau's fall from grace seemingly accelerated while we were distracted by the global health issues that began in the spring of 2020. The corresponding changes in US political norms and social practices during this time probably also had some effect on the FBI; however, those effects are yet to be quantified, assessed, and reported (if they ever will be).

I am confident that there will be some rebuttals from people who recently departed FBI service or who are currently managing FBI operations. I can appreciate their viewpoints. Maybe some individuals will feel that the bureau was and still is without fault. If so, a lack of critical self-assessment could possibly be a causal factor in the bureau's current problem set. I also anticipate strongly worded justifications for some questionable actions and choices in recent history. Again, I can appreciate such viewpoints. In contrast, I also expect some silent nods of approval and murmurs of concurrence over the observations provided in this book. I also expect there could be some personal attacks and some denigration of my career. I welcome all perspectives, and we will have to see where the conversation goes.

Throughout this book, I offered my personal views and experiences about the different phases of my professional career. I intended no malice toward anyone, but I will always be willing to talk about certain FBI-related subjects that may be considered radioactive to those who are still connected to the organization—personally, professionally, or financially. That said, I am still holding on to what the FBI was to me and what it could be again.

Managing Cultural Challenge and Change

I saw the FBI senior leadership environment changing as I departed. From what I have been told by some of my former colleagues who remained with the bureau or in touch with the bureau, I am not sure that much of anything has improved. FBI special agents in charge have been subjected to a perceived lack of support from FBIHQ, and a growing number have felt that the bureau was becoming overly politicized in how it addressed polarizing issues. FBI whistleblowers have gained national exposure in telling their stories before congressional committees, and others have gained a presence in the media due to their resignations in protest over what they felt were questionable practices. Anecdotally, I received informal accounts of excessive egos, micromanagement, bad decision-making, inconsistent leadership, mission distraction, and other factors that could have caused some of the bureau's emergent challenges.

In addition to the aforementioned factors, the FBI has been publicly accused of losing its investigative objectivity and political impartiality in the questionable handling of certain laptops, reported surveillance of school parents, and perceived treatment of former US presidents. In various open-source media and social media channels, some parties have felt that the FBI has adopted heavy-handed tactics against conservative-leaning individuals. I occasionally watch televised congressional testimonies from FBI senior executives and am sometimes puzzled by the instances when these executives display a lack of preparation or a combative tone with congressional members. I have been concerned about seeing calls from political figures for the FBI to be defunded or even abolished. As I noted earlier, I wondered what happened to my FBI, and after some personal deliberation, I decided to commit my thoughts to writing despite my reservations.

For a more objective conversation, I selected a few situations that I felt were symptomatic of the FBI's actual or perceived decline in leadership effectiveness and operational excellence.

The first situation for discussion is the 2018 school shooting tragedy in Parkland, Florida. Note that this discussion was not based on any specific FBI report but was generated from my personal recall of the situation and open-source research regarding the events leading up to and outcomes subsequent to the shooting event.

In the two following situations, I based my thoughts on past notable reviews of FBI activities by the Department of Justice (DOJ), and the Office of the Inspector General (OIG). Readers should know that DOJ-OIG reports, when unclassified, are available for public review at the DOJ website. I selected what I felt were two impactful reports for discussion and review. These reports were the DOJ-OIG's investigation of the FBI's handling of allegations of sexual abuse by former USA gymnastics physician Lawrence Gerard Nassar; and the "Durham Report," published by Special Counsel John H. Durham, about Crossfire Hurricane intelligence and investigative activities arising out of the 2016 presidential campaign.

The Marjory Stoneman Douglas High School Shooting

Immediately after the Marjory Stoneman Douglas High School shooting in Parkland, Florida, on February 14, 2018, the FBI discovered that it had previously received contact from a family member of the shooter through its public access tip line. This family member warned that the shooter could possibly do something along the lines of what happened in Parkland. The FBI personnel involved in processing the tip line did not take action on the call, as it did not meet established response protocols that prevailed at the time. As I initially reviewed the situation, I saw an absence of investigative curiosity and a surprising lack of follow-up. Possible causal factors included weak or distracted leadership, untrained junior staff members, or inadequate or outdated protocols. We later found that it was a dynamic combination of these factors, which was not confirmed until the FBI's role in the Parkland incident was closely reviewed. The after-action reviews and causal analyses conducted by the STB and the FBI's Inspection Division prompted a multitude of organizational changes in bureau policy to improve the responsiveness in the prevailing threat environment. But the damage was already done to the victims, their families, and the FBI brand. No amount of after-action review, critique, and corrective action could undo what had happened.

Fidelity, Bravery, and Integrity—What Happened?

As an EAD with strategic FBIHQ oversight for the public access program that received contacts from our communities, I did not have access to this program's daily operations or mission execution but began an earnest review of what occurred. While we were sorting it all out, one of the immediate responses we received from the public access program personnel was this somewhat insufficient response: "We were following our policies." I was horrified and had to explain to the director and deputy director how this shortfall occurred. At this point, the director had been in his role for only a short time, but people were calling for his resignation. The deputy director was called to testify on the Hill regarding this matter, as our national leaders wanted answers. So, the mighty FBI was brought to its knees by the decisions of relatively junior personnel who could not have foreseen the impact of their actions. One of the primary areas for concern from my view was that the FBI was no longer conducting business in an environment where it was able to simply say that it was following policies when a shortfall occurred, and lives were lost.

As I learned to do earlier in my career, I worked with the STB executive staff, sought out information, conducted logical investigative actions, gathered available information, and began the long march into the pre- and post-worlds of the FBI's role in the events leading up to the Parkland tragedy. After a number of conversations with program managers and FBI executives, I found that we experienced breakdowns in the areas of program leadership, procedural execution, emerging threat management, and organizational accountability. Without going into too much detail for this discussion, the FBI personnel involved could have been seen as not properly fulfilling their assigned duties and as having missed an opportunity to potentially interdict actions that led to the Parkland shooting. Everyone we spoke with was devastated, but that did not matter. When queried, the FBI managers said that they followed their policies (which might not have been 100 percent true). They also did not feel that they were personally accountable for the Parkland shooting (which I agreed with to a point). Upon demand, they showed us their working policies and standard operating procedures, which amounted to incoherent piles of outdated, miscellaneous documents that were not adequate on any level; so much for following policy as a justification for what happened in FBI channels.

The previously accepted approach of "following policy" was also an absolute failure for the school resource officer who was on scene at the Marjory Stoneman School during the shooting. This officer did not enter the school to engage the shooter in line with reported legacy policies and practices. By relying on the practice of taking a defensive position outside of the school and waiting for backup, more lives were likely lost while responding police officers made their way to the school.

I could probably write a short book specifically on the topic of Parkland and the FBI's part of this tragedy, but I will leave this discussion where it is for now. That said, it remains unclear if the FBI could have prevented the Parkland tragedy—but we certainly could have tried harder. If we had engaged this matter with greater leadership and investigative assertiveness, the FBI might have had a chance to interact with the shooter and his family before the event to possibly change his behavior. We could have possibly alerted our Parkland law enforcement partners to the shooter's behavior and the family member's warning call. We could have asked the partners to contact the family and speak directly with the shooter for possible intervention. (The Parkland shooter was known to local law enforcement through previous interactions.) Maybe we could have gotten him some help and spared the lives of the Parkland victims. This is a lot of what-ifs, could haves, and hindsight questions with no real answers. That was not the FBI way that I had been schooled in, and I knew we had to do better.

I knew then that the FBI had to implement new assessment criteria to determine if we were doing our jobs properly, despite our usual dependence on legacy policies and practices. Blind dependency and rote execution based on legacy policies and practices in the FBI's line of work, while normally preferred, could have led to the development of bureaucratic indifference and/or complacency in our public access program. We have all suffered from the effects of bureaucratic indifference and/or complacency—when people do not care about excellence and simply comply with policies and procedures at the lowest levels required to get by. We have all fallen victim to people who give the minimum effort to meet the letter of an established policy as opposed to fulfilling the spirit of superior mission achievement and professionalism. In my view, bureaucratic indifference and/or complacency remain the primary disease of most governmental functions and could have been silent contributors in this tragedy.

Three Areas for Quick Assessment

I looked deeply into the FBI's part in the Parkland situation. I talked at length with my executive staff about how we, at the STB, were going to change the methods by which we would evaluate ourselves leading up to, during, and in the aftermath of any crises or critical situations. I laid out three general assessment points:

1. What were we **required** to do in line with applicable laws, regulations, and policies?

2. What **should** we have done to properly manage the situation?
3. What was **expected** of us by our national leaders and the American public?

While these assessment areas could be relatively simple (which was the point), they could potentially yield different, if not conflicting, complex outcomes. When conflicts occurred in discussions, we would see increased complexity in determining if we planned properly or if we took or would take the proper actions. Ultimately, when planning, training, and then responding to the mission environment, we had to be confident that we would make the right choices or at least have the right thought processes. We had to look at the leadership, the other people involved, and the threat or situation at hand. We had to take a hard look at ourselves with no egos or ass-covering and determine if we were ready for anything. In the following discussion, I will apply the assessment points (in a general fashion) to the actions of the on-scene school resource officer during the Parkland tragedy.

Assessment Point 1: What were we required to do in line with applicable laws, regulations, and policies?

In the Parkland matter, the on-scene school resource officer reportedly did not know where the shots were coming from and chose to not enter the school. From a strict protocol matter, the officer did not follow the post-Columbine training protocol that called for immediate engagement. However, the Broward County Sheriff's Office policy during the 2018 Parkland shooting reportedly stated that deputies "**may**" confront active shooters, not that they "**shall**." This suggestive instead of directive wording allowed the on-site Parkland school resource officer to justify not entering the building during the shooting. In 2019, the officer was charged with several counts related to his actions during the shooting:

- Seven counts of neglect of a child
- Three counts of culpable negligence
- One count of perjury

When the trial ended, the school resource officer was found not guilty on all counts.

Assessment Point 2: What should we have done to properly manage the situation?

Our hindsight assessment brings us to what the on-scene officer should have done as a law enforcement professional and protector. In most after-action discussion I heard on this matter, I sensed that everyone, from citizen to law enforcement officer to public leader, expected the school resource officer to enter the school and engage, distract, or defeat the shooter before backup arrived. I agree, and not much more can be added. I wonder how much training the on-scene officer had received in making the kind of confrontation that people expected. I also wonder what kind of warrior/protector culture the parent organization promoted and maintained in dealing with such matters.

Assessment Point 3: What was expected of us by our national leaders and the American public?

As a sworn law enforcement officer in today's world, this might have been a time when a sacrificial engagement would have been expected to save at least some of those who perished that day. I am not saying that is definitively the proper textbook tactical approach, but in light of this and other school shooting incidents, an aggressive engagement with the shooter was likely expected by the public and our governing officials. Ultimately, the law enforcement officer on scene was not bold in entering the school building, but followed established policy, and people died.

We will see in the following chapter how this three-step assessment approach could have been implemented in a post-mortem performance evaluation of the FBI's handling of the Olympic athlete sexual abuse case.

"What happened to the FBI that allowed this tragedy to develop over time?"

16

THE FBI'S HANDLING OF THE OLYMPIC GYMNAST SEXUAL ABUSE CASE

The FBI's handling of this matter, formally designated by the DOJ Office of the Inspector General as "Investigation and Review of the Federal Bureau of Investigation's Handling of Allegations of Sexual Abuse by Former USA Gymnastics Physician Lawrence Gerard Nassar," is a prime example of how FBI operations could go very wrong. For this matter, the Indianapolis Field Office spectacularly failed to properly manage numerous allegations of sexual abuse by former USA Gymnastics physician Lawrence Nassar.

This case was evidence of the ways that the FBI had declined in its traditional leadership approach and operational excellence. In a word, this case was a debacle. It was a convergence of failed leadership, bad decision-making, ineptitude, integrity shortfalls, and case management deficiencies that allowed young women to be abused over time despite numerous complaints to the FBI and other officials. Where was the fabled fidelity, bravery, and integrity that once influenced people to seek out the bureau for help when the victims felt no one else could be trusted? Where was the skilled investigative response that previously characterized FBI operations?

Put bluntly, this case was an embarrassment. What happened to the FBI that allowed this tragedy to develop over time?

The DOJ-OIG's Review of the FBI's Handling of the Nassar Case

The following excerpt is from the DOJ-OIG's review of the FBI's handling of the Nassar case. It is but a small portion of the assessment, but it serves as a summary of the OIG's findings:

> The OIG found that, despite the extraordinarily serious nature of the allegations and the possibility that Nassar's conduct could be continuing, senior officials in the FBI Indianapolis Field Office failed to respond to the Nassar allegations with the utmost seriousness and urgency that they deserved and required, made numerous and fundamental errors when they did respond to them, and violated multiple FBI policies. The Indianapolis Field Office did not undertake any investigative activity until September 2—five weeks after the meeting with USA Gymnastics—when they telephonically interviewed one of the three athletes. Further, FBI Indianapolis never interviewed the other two gymnasts who they were told were available to meet with FBI investigators. This absence of any serious investigative activity was compounded when the Indianapolis Field Office did not transfer the matter to the FBI office (the Lansing Resident Agency), where venue most likely would have existed had evidence been developed to support the potential federal crimes being considered, even though the Indianapolis office had been advised to do so by the USAO and had told USA Gymnastics that the transfer

had occurred. Additionally, the Indianapolis office did not notify state or local authorities of the sexual assault allegations even though it questioned whether there was federal jurisdiction to pursue them. As a result, the Lansing Resident Agency did not learn of the Nassar allegations until over a year after they were first reported to the FBI and then learned of them only from the MSUPD [Michigan State University Police Department]. Moreover, the FBI conducted no investigative activity in the matter for more than 8 months following the September 2015 interview. During that period of time, as alleged and detailed in numerous civil complaints, Nassar's sexual assaults continued.

Further, when the FBI's handling of the Nassar matter came under scrutiny from the public, Congress, the media, and FBI headquarters in 2017 and 2018, Indianapolis officials did not take responsibility for their failures. Instead, they provided incomplete and inaccurate information in response to FBI internal inquiries (and Abbott [Special Agent in Charge], after he retired, provided inaccurate information to the media) to make it appear that the Indianapolis office had been diligent in its follow-up efforts and they did so, in part, by blaming others for their own failures........ In addition, we concluded that the Indianapolis SSA, in an effort to minimize or excuse his errors, made false statements during two OIG-compelled interviews regarding his interview of one of Nassar's victims. Similarly, we found that Abbott, in an effort to minimize or excuse his own and his office's actions, falsely asserted in two separate OIG interviews that he communicated with both the Detroit SAC and the Los

Angeles SAC about the Nassar allegations and sent ECs to both field offices in the fall of 2015. We found no evidence to support these claims…….. These failures by Indianapolis officials contributed to a delay of over a year in the proper FBI field office and local authorities initiating investigations that ultimately determined that Nassar had engaged in widespread sexual assaults of over 100 victims and possessed child pornography, led to convictions in both federal and state court, and resulted in jail sentences totaling over 100 years. In addition, we concluded that the Indianapolis SSA ultimately drafted an interview summary 17 months after the interview of Gymnast 1 that contained materially false statements and omitted material information.

Basically, the DOJ-OIG found that the FBI failed in responding to the claims of the sexual abuse victims on all counts. We will see shortfalls in this Indianapolis case that are similar to the Parkland matter. There were similar breakdowns in program leadership, procedural execution, emerging threat management, and organizational accountability. According to the DOJ-OIG, the Indianapolis Field Office investigators and managers did not follow established procedures or uphold standards in how FBI cases are conducted and managed. There was no sense of urgency or follow-up on the complaints filed by the victims. The DOJ-OIG found delays in action that allowed the abuse to continue. From my view, how could this situation be seen as anything other than a result of ineptitude and bureaucratic indifference? As a career FBI special agent, I was greatly shamed over this matter.

Looking back at my earlier experiences when I served as a FBIHQ program manager, field office squad supervisor, field office ASAC, and field office SAC during my FBI career, I was floored by the nature of this case and how poorly it was handled. I immediately began thinking about what causal factors were present without considering the personalities of the people immediately involved. I also thought about the proportionality of malice versus ineptitude that developed during this case. Were those involved really that bad as people, or were they really that bad at their jobs, or maybe some of each?

As I wondered how this could have happened, I thought back to my time as the SAC for the Buffalo Field Office. I thought that the circumstances surrounding the Nassar case could have occurred in Buffalo had that office been exposed to the same environmental factors before we changed the Buffalo leadership approach and operational model. I looked back at my arrival in Buffalo and recalled the laxity in leadership, the absence of a sense of urgency, and the generally weak organizational culture. I also recalled the inconsistent sense of warriorship and protectorship that the office initially displayed. We changed it in Buffalo, but we had to first acknowledge our faults and work to do better. And we did so for the American people. Unfortunately, my former colleagues in Indianapolis were not able to self-correct and could not save the Nassar victims from further abuse.

Causal Inventory and Evaluation

After a brief review of the Nassar DOJ-OIG findings, I developed the following causal inventory based upon my professional experiences, insights, senior agent mentorship, and FBI training. This inventory will build context in areas in which the FBI should be seeking deep self-assessment and aggressive corrective action. These factors can also be adapted for and applied to any other organizations that are experiencing performance difficulties:

Definitive Causal Factors for the Nassar Case:
- Lax leadership culture
- Breakdown in holding standards
- Absence of effective program oversight and program management
- Line supervisory incompetence
- Absence of case agent ownership
- Absence of investigative curiosity and rigor
- Bureaucratic indifference—acceptance of compliance versus promotion of high-performance
- Missing or unclear senior leadership intent and expectations

Possible Additional Factors for the Nassar Case:
- Overall decline of FBI organizational culture—tolerated field office mediocrity
- Lack of initiative (part of a defective culture local to the Indianapolis Field Office)
- Presence of personal interests that impacted investigative direction
- Absence of adequate FBIHQ program instruction/direction
- Lack of meaningful training/skill building for supervisors and case agents
- Integrity gaps
- Bravery gaps
- Leadership timidity due to not wanting to be labeled a "micromanager"
- Desire by leadership to be liked versus being operationally astute and effective

I am sure that other micro-factors could be added to the inventory, but the overall message is that these, and possibly other, substandard practices converged to make the Nassar investigation a complete disaster. This convergence resulted in the extended suffering of a group of victims at the hands of an abuser, who occupied a position of trust. The practices, principles, and values that I learned from my old breed senior agent mentors were violated or not executed at all. The lack of adherence to the FBI's proven practices contributed directly to the disaster. We will apply the three-point assessment developed during the Parkland tragedy to the Nassar case to see how FBI Indianapolis fared.

Applying the Three-Point Assessment to the Nassar Case

Using the three-point assessment model from the Parkland shooting tragedy, we will review and assess the Nassar case to see if the FBI measured up, and if not, why not. We will summarize the factors here:

Assessment Point 1: What were we required to do in line with applicable laws, regulations, and policies?

From an FBI policy and practice perspective (the legal issues speak for themselves), a case of this type and potential magnitude should have been briefed to the Indianapolis SAC on a weekly to biweekly basis, with the program ASAC, cognizant supervisory special agent (squad supervisor), and the case agent(s) providing reports on what had been accomplished and what was planned for the next working period. Similar reports could have also been provided to FBIHQ program managers to maintain situational awareness and seek guidance where applicable. I used to do these types of "top case" reviews when I was an SAC to keep me connected to the programs. I am not sure what the briefing cycles actually were, but it did not appear that this important management practice was properly executed if it was executed at all.

In addition, an inventory of issues and action items (known inside the FBI as a "tickler system") should have been covered during meetings to keep certain matters front and center for follow-up and resolution by specific deadlines or timelines. I used to maintain an inventory of action items, tasks, and timelines for every meeting so we could monitor issues for satisfactory resolution by certain deadlines. During such periodic updates, the Indianapolis SAC could have provided instructions for his team while looking for ways to work through barriers and challenges with his senior executives. In the end, an integrated investigative approach and a common operating perspective could/should have been set and maintained for all levels of the investigative team.

The SAC should have set up a unified chain of command with clear direction and a briefing and reporting structure. This model, adopted in alignment with the FBI's file review policies, could have ensured that this case was either properly executed in Indianapolis or transferred to another field office for proper resolution. If I were able to perform a direct after-action review of the Nassar matter, I would have examined the files to determine whether or not the case management and documentation were in line with established FBI standards. I am not confident that a favorable review would have resulted.

Assessment Point 2: What should we have done to properly manage the situation?

I am curious about whether the Indianapolis Field Office leaders ever sat down during this investigation and asked themselves what they should have been doing, as opposed to simply checking procedural boxes (or not) and complying with minimum administrative requirements (which they did not seem to do well). Were those leaders merely fulfilling their bureaucratic obligations, or were they outraged as societal protectors by the reported transgressions of the person accused of violating young women? Was the FBI going through the motions, or were they working tirelessly to remove a menace from the midst of these vulnerable women?

It appears that the Indianapolis leaders failed to ask themselves the basic question of what they should have been doing as opposed to what they were required to do. If you review the entire DOJ-OIG report on this matter, you will see various accounts of incompetence, but you will also see shortfalls in the fidelity, bravery, and integrity that had always been associated with the FBI. This case should have been an SAC priority matter, and case agents should have been working on it as if their own children were living in such an environment of danger and mistreatment. What should have been the epitome of a well-orchestrated, high-energy, skilled investigative effort eventually became a source of frustration and harm for the victims and embarrassment for the FBI. The victims and associated stakeholders deserved a well-coordinated effort among FBI field offices, FBIHQ, and state and local authorities to swiftly mitigate the threat of further abuse and aggressively place the abuser into the hands of officials for prosecution. All of the points noted in this and the prior assessment point should have been done in accordance with FBI standards. Unfortunately, none of this happened.

Assessment Point 3: What was expected of us by our national leaders and the American public?

As in the Parkland matter, the public and our governing officials expected a strong, skilled, timely investigative response from the law enforcement community, especially from the FBI. The public expected and the victims deserved an energized FBI response with the best case agents available working on the matter as aggressively as circumstances allowed. The victims expected the best in protection and support that the bureau could offer. Everyone rightly expected strict adherence to investigative protocols that would pave the way to a swift and successful prosecution. In addition, all parties expected that the FBI would coordinate investigative and administrative activities in its internal channels to ensure proper case management between different venues. However, none of these things were done well—and some were not at all—as evidenced by the OIG findings. This investigation should have become a case study and a cautionary tale for the rest of the organization. Outside of punishing the people who failed so miserably, did the FBI learn anything about applicable practices that could be reinforced in meeting the expectations of our national leaders and the American public? It is hard to tell, but it is doubtful.

As in previous instances throughout my career, I was concerned about the absence of warrior spirit, protectorship, and ownership that should have been visibly present to properly pursue this kind of investigation. How did the Indianapolis Field Office become so bureaucratically indifferent, and how long had such a defective culture been in place? Where was the investigative fire in resolving this issue in an effective manner? Where were the FBI dragonslayers to protect these young women? The victims called the FBI directly for help, and I was sad to see the inept, indifferent reaction. I saw one of the macro contributors to failure in this matter as a declining FBI culture, which allowed a climate of mediocrity to develop and permitted an organizational failure of monumental proportion.

A few closing thoughts on this matter.

What did the FBI leadership do to ensure this kind of failure could never happen again? Hard to tell. The OIG provided recommendations to the FBI on clarifying its policies and training its staff members. This type of approach is a non-solution (and almost always has been). This type of approach just leads to more bureaucratic nonsense. The FBI does not need a slew of additional guidance documents, legal policy clarifications, and compliance reviews to add to the current mountain of such useless administrative nonsense. These acts of administrative contrition simply take up time without delivering a measurable, beneficial outcome. As for training, I am definitely in favor of providing instruction that actually builds the skills, knowledge, and cultural values that can be applied to the operating environment. I am not talking about more online nonsensical ethics awareness training courses. The FBI already has a glut of this kind of garbage that has, at best, delivered inconsistent results. Adding more bureaucratic ass-covering is not a solution to get people to perform their duties in a skilled, principled manner. Training and ass-covering cannot resolve a cultural problem.

As with simply adding training, implementing mindless layers of review/approval and more non-value-added policies is not helpful unless previous policies are found to be deficient and new policies are not made overly restrictive, which is often the case in penance-based solutions. I have seen where the combination of excessively restrictive policy, time-consuming training, and layers upon layers of approval can paralyze organizations. For example, FBI case agents have the benefit of the Domestic Investigations and Operations Guide (DIOG), a roughly 1,000-page policy paperweight that created a procedural minefield and made agents risk-averse and afraid of getting into trouble for "compliance issues." When the DIOG came about, we were not remaking the fabled FBI special agents of old who feared little and sometimes got into a bit of difficulty for doing what was right. Personally, I do not think I saw an instance where the DIOG provided benefit to case agent morale and investigative assertiveness. In fact, I saw many instances of the opposite.

Finally, according to the DOJ-OIG findings, FBI Indianapolis Field Office leadership personnel tried to blame others and possibly lied to cover up their own incompetence or dereliction. That was the most disappointing shortfall that I saw. No fidelity, bravery, or integrity to be found there. The office failed on every level—the people, programs, and systems involved in the Nassar case appeared to be deficient. The bigger bureau failed in allowing this flawed environment to exist in the Indianapolis Field Office. The FBI brand was damaged, and confidence was eroded in the hearts of our national leaders and the American public. One has to wonder if the FBI learned from this unfortunate situation. It did not seem so.

" In retrospect, Crossfire could have easily become a case study on how **NOT** to conduct an investigation. While it was never made into an instructive case study, it did serve as the basis for changes to how FBIHQ could or would manage sensitive investigative operations in the future. "

17

THE DURHAM REPORT—SUMMARY ASSESSMENT

The Durham Report, provided by Special Counsel John H. Durham in May 2023, provided an assessment of one of the FBI's most well-known investigations, Crossfire Hurricane (hereafter Crossfire). This case became famous, or infamous, in how it affected the FBI and its image. FBI careers ended or were damaged, and our nation suffered embarrassment for the antics that potentially sought to influence our political processes.

Crossfire Hurricane

Crossfire was an FBI national security investigation that was initiated to determine if a sitting president of the United States might have had a relationship with a foreign government that was harmful to our country. This snake-bit investigation fomented the end of several FBI careers, including the FBI director, deputy director, a deputy assistant director, and other FBI officials.

In retrospect, Crossfire could have easily become a case study on how **NOT** to conduct an investigation. While it was never made into an instructive case study, it did serve as the basis for changes to how FBIHQ could or would manage sensitive investigative operations in the future. Some of the same shortfalls and causal factors that were previously found in the Parkland matter and the Indianapolis Field Office Nassar case were present in Crossfire, albeit in different incarnations. As such, it did not appear that the FBI actually learned its lesson after the Nassar case concluded.

Here is an excerpt from Special Counsel Durham's report that summarizes the nature of his findings:

> The objective facts show that the FBI's handling of important aspects of the Crossfire Hurricane matter were seriously deficient. Some FBI employees who were interviewed by our investigators advised that they had significant reservations about aspects of Crossfire Hurricane and tried to convey their misgivings to their superiors. Others had doubts about the investigation, but did not voice their concerns. In some cases, nothing was said because of a sense that there had to be more compelling information in the possession of those closest to the decision-making center of the case than had been made known to them. And there were still other current and former employees who maintained that they did the best they could to take reasonable investigative steps and acted within the FBI's various policies, procedures, and guidelines. As the more complete record now shows, there are specific areas of Crossfire Hurricane activity in which the FBI badly underperformed and failed, not only in its duties to the public, but also in preventing the severe reputational harm that has befallen the FBI as a consequence of Crossfire Hurricane. Importantly, had the Crossfire Hurricane actors faithfully followed their own principles regarding objectivity and integrity, there were clear opportunities to have avoided the mistakes and to have

The Durham Report—Summary Assessment

prevented the damage resulting from their embrace of seriously flawed information that they failed to analyze and assess properly....... One of the chief errors from the start of Crossfire Hurricane was the poor analysis the FBI brought to bear on the critical pieces of information that it had gathered, as well as an overreliance on flawed or incomplete human intelligence that only later was found to be plainly unreliable........ Given the foregoing, and viewing the facts in a light most favorable to the Crossfire Hurricane investigators, it seems highly likely that, at a minimum, confirmation bias played a significant role in the FBI's acceptance of extraordinarily serious allegations derived from uncorroborated information that had not been subjected to the typical exacting analysis employed by the FBI and other members of the Intelligence Community. In short, it is the Office's assessment that the FBI discounted or willfully ignored material information that did not support the narrative of a collusive relationship between Trump and Russia. Similarly, the FBI Inspection Division Report says that the investigators "repeatedly ignore[d] or explain[ed] away evidence contrary to the theory the Trump campaign ...... had conspired with Russia .... It appeared that ...... there was a pattern of assuming nefarious intent."[1749] An objective and honest assessment of these strands of information should have caused the FBI to question not only the predication for Crossfire Hurricane, but also to reflect on whether the FBI was being manipulated for political or other purposes. Unfortunately, it did not.

Crossfire Hurricane Discussion and Evaluation

The Durham Report was instrumental in shedding light on how Crossfire reflected many of the continuing symptoms of FBI cultural erosion and performance decline in key areas. The following review of the Crossfire investigation can serve as a baseline in generating points for additional discussion and associated evaluation about the FBI's future:

- **Political, ideological, and relationship-driven operations took precedence without an opposing view or an objective oversight body:** In hindsight, it appears that the primary FBI Crossfire protagonists held similar political leanings and congruent ideologies about the 2016 election, its candidates, and the outcome. When this group of like-minded people was assembled, it did not require much influence to align with each other and seek to please the boss in a real or perceived manner. (I have seen this same phenomenon occur in certain unrelated FBI meetings and activities.) The deputy assistant director who led the Crossfire investigation appeared to substitute his own personal beliefs and political leanings for historically objective FBI investigative procedures and protocols. At this point, it is safe to say that the senior members of the Crossfire team were not pleased with the outcome of the 2016 presidential election and appeared to lose their objectivity while conducting the investigation. It is possible that, in their own view, they became historic figures who were on a mission to save the US from destruction at the hands of a newly elected president (whom they apparently did not approve of).
- **Departure from traditional FBI investigative oversight and leadership structures:** The deputy director

should not have been given direct oversight for the investigation—he has too much to watch across the entire organization to be closely managing this kind of case. The FBI deputy director's role is one of vast organizational responsibility and accountability, as he oversees all operational and investigative activities—domestic and abroad—that the bureau participates in. He is the highest-ranking career senior executive service member in the organization (the director is a political appointee). He serves as the operations chief for all fifty-six field offices and as overseer of all substantial investigative issues that arise, and he is everyone's boss, on some level, for the entire FBI rank and file. The deputy director's office is also accountable for setting policy for the organization, overseeing all investigations, approving administrative processes, and serving as the FBI director's primary advisor for strategic operations. As such, expecting him to serve as the direct overseer and manager of the Crossfire investigation was a recipe for disappointment. The proven, traditional FBI case oversight structure could have provided improved levels of supervision, compliance management, and investigative steerage (remember those file reviews). The FBI's case file review process seemed to be missing or incomplete at best. As mentioned previously, this process is one of the most basic duties of a supervisory special agent in which a review of pending investigative case files is conducted in a prescribed schedule (usually ninety-day intervals or shorter when warranted). This process mandates that case agents update their files and meet with their supervisors to ensure compliance, gauge investigative progress, and determine next steps. It is also an opportunity for supervisors to counsel agents when gaps or shortfalls are discovered. A properly observed file review process could have possibly saved the Crossfire investigation. For example, the deputy assistant director in charge of the Crossfire investigation was authoring and approving his own communications, which is a strongly discouraged practice in FBI operations. Files reviews could have identified this and other substandard practices and provided corrective instruction.

- **Absence of FBIHQ Criminal Investigative Division involvement:** Participation from this operational division, even on a limited basis, could have helped the FBI focus on the possible presence of criminal activity and maintain awareness of potential future criminal proceedings. Granted, this was primarily a counterintelligence case, but input from FBI criminal investigators could have enhanced the entire Crossfire operation and prevented some of the groupthink-related shortfalls noted by the Durham Report. The criminal program investigators could have counterbalanced the counterintelligence approaches, possibly shed light on investigative gaps, and mitigated the development of confirmation bias as noted by Special Counsel Durham.

- **The legal counsel assigned to the Crossfire investigation reported directly to the deputy director and wielded his authority by proxy:** The legal counsel was tough and smart and had a good command of the legal issues at hand; however, her direct line to the deputy director allowed her to overly influence operational decision-making. She served in a quasi-managerial capacity outside of her GS-15 grade as a line attorney. She had more decision-making influence than was warranted and drifted away from providing objective legal counsel. This attorney was allowed to function in a manner similar to SES-level operations managers in making administrative and operational decisions that impacted the Crossfire investigation. This type of phenomenon with FBI attorneys had evolved from the days following the September 11th tragedy, when FBIHQ operations managers became much more risk-averse in making decisions. These operations managers began to excessively defer to the Office of General Counsel (the bureau's internal attorney cadre) to weigh in on and approve decisions—possibly to avoid blame or to share accountability for risky decisions that might have possibly led to negative outcomes. The FBI attorneys soon began telling operational managers what they could or could not do, and investigative personnel soon were required to obtain attorney reviews/approvals for certain case-related actions that were not actually matters of legality. For the Crossfire investigation, this substandard operating model could have been avoided if the deputy director did not directly oversee the investigation or if he had more clearly drawn out the roles and responsibilities among operations leaders and legal counsel.

- **FBIHQ direct oversight and operation of national security investigations:** This practice had not been a normal approach prior to September 11, 2001. This product of the post–September 11th environment was an indicator of FBIHQ's lowered trust and confidence in field office operations. In fact, overall confidence in the entire FBI hit historically low points after September 11th, and the preference for central command and control became favored by the director and other senior leaders. FBIHQ wanted to directly oversee and manage casework, but it was not properly set up to do. It had no system for conducting file reviews or coordinating the use of field office manpower and resources to complete such reviews. The FBIHQ oversight and case management model quickly became a burden to field offices and was seen primarily as a way to feed the executive briefing machine. FBIHQ had drifted into a habit of driving field office investigative operational tempo from Washington, DC, by directing investigative objectives and requiring a variety of resource-draining activities. These activities included FISA court-authorized technical and twenty-four-hour physical surveillance operations where field office managers sometimes questioned the value. In the end, FBIHQ had no business directly managing investigations, and the difficulties eventually encountered during the Crossfire investigation further reinforced the importance of keeping investigations in the field offices and adding temporary duty resources or enhanced FBIHQ oversight as required.

- **Absence of a philosophical counterbalance to promote and sustain objectivity:** There were simply too many like-minded people in charge or who were highly influential in the Crossfire investigation. The primary Crossfire protagonists appeared to possess similar political leanings, personal values, and desired investigative outcomes. The Durham Report confirms the presence of bias. This high level of ideological commonality in the Crossfire team might have stifled opposing dialogues that could have promoted improved levels of objectivity and counterbalancing views. The cultivation of competing views might have prevented certain assumptions from dominating the primary investigation. A sense of groupthink among Crossfire managers and participants seemed to dominate and stifle investigative curiosity and objectivity. This groupthink could have unwittingly advanced the preference for certain practices and results that were aligned with the political or personal beliefs of the Crossfire leadership team.

- **Incomplete investigative model and gaps in due diligence:** The Durham Report's citing of bias within the Crossfire team, the speed of its investigative efforts, and the potential impact of outcomes may have unduly impacted the due diligence that had always defined FBI casework. Also, it seemed that the potential historical impact of the Crossfire investigation may have created adrenaline-based decision-making and hasty planning perspectives that were not well vetted or only partially executed. The absence of interviews with key persons of interest and the lack of validation of basic investigative details showed that the work being done was not up to traditional FBI standards. It appeared that Crossfire senior leadership was not adequately checking investigative results for quality and completeness. Shortfalls in leadership, emotional objectivity, and case oversight were primary contributors to the failure of the Crossfire investigation. Participants in the Crossfire investigation were possibly overcome by the potential historical gravity of their work. There did not seem to be any guardrails in place to ensure that emotions and personal agendas did not take precedence over objective, procedure-driven investigative practices. This drift toward acting on emotions rather than on investigative rigor and objective fact-gathering is another

sign of a probable decline in the FBI's leadership and investigative cultures. Were there excessive egos in play or shortfalls in professionalism? It may have been a combination of both. We may never know for sure.
- **Use of non-secure, dedicated investigative communications:** A number of personal exchanges and undisciplined interactions among Crossfire personnel were combined with investigation-related communications. This practice led to public scrutiny and the unfavorable exposure of personal relationships, politically based perspectives, and sensitive investigative activities. The personal nature of some Crossfire senior team members' communications ultimately led to embarrassment for the FBI and the people involved and resulted in a general decline in the bureau's perceived objectivity and investigative credibility.

Ultimately, the Durham Report's assessment of the FBI's performance in the Crossfire investigation led to increased doubt and discomfort among national leaders and the American public in these areas:

- Leadership practices
- Trustworthiness and credibility
- Competence and judgment
- Investigative and administrative methodologies
- Objectivity and impartiality
- Transparency

The Durham Report purposely did not prescribe ways for the FBI to remedy the performance and compliance shortfalls, but the bureau should have used the report to take a hard look at itself and determine its general health and welfare.

When All Was Said and Done

Some people criticized the Durham Report because it was either not what they thought it was or what they thought it should be. This report should not be seen as a 360-degree, 100-percent solution for identifying and resolving the issues that surrounded the Crossfire investigation. Special Counsel Durham was closing up shop at the conclusion of his review, and he used the published report to summarize his findings and to present his work to the public.

After the Durham Report was published, some in the media and Congress were unhappy because no one was arrested. As for the impact of the Crossfire investigation to FBI personnel, Director Comey and Deputy Director McCabe were fired from their positions but were not subjected to legal action by DOJ. The counterintelligence deputy assistant director, who was in charge of the Crossfire investigation, was fired from the FBI with no legal penalty. The FBI OGC attorney who served as counsel to the deputy director resigned and left the FBI without legal penalty. Aside from a separate FBI general counsel line attorney who was prosecuted for altering documentation (but is reportedly back in law practice), the primary overseers of the Crossfire investigation were not found to have acted in ways that were considered criminal in nature.

Politically influenced? Likely.
Unethical? Maybe.
Incompetent? Perhaps.
Outside of FBI policy and standards? Probably.
Maybe all of these things.
What happened to my FBI?

> Among the perceived wreckage, there was much about the FBI that was still good and salvageable; however, much of the pre–September 11th FBI was discarded or left to atrophy to make way for the new FBI.

18

CULTURAL CHANGES AND EFFECTS ON LEADERSHIP

Throughout this book, the topics of culture and leadership have been raised as causal factors in the FBI's challenges. As such, a discussion on where some of these challenges began during my tenure could be helpful in understanding how they happened.

Post-9/11 Practices and the Impact to FBI Culture

After September 11, 2001, the federal government encountered waves of evaluation and re-evaluation about perceived and actual failures in how its applicable agencies conducted business leading up to that terrible day. As a result, Congress mandated that intelligence community (primarily the FBI) adopt new practices to resolve identified shortfalls and operational failures. In the eyes of many, the FBI had to learn how to "connect the dots" to fill recognized intelligence gaps. To meet a host of new and expanding national security and public safety needs, the bureau reacted to congressional calls for change by building new investigative programs, expanding national security capabilities, and improving analytical capacities. These actions alone would not prove to be sufficient in appeasing national leadership. Congressional leaders also called for the implementation of new practices that would transform the FBI from the previous reactive, cops-and-robbers culture to a new model based on predictive, preventive, intelligence-informed domestic security operations.

During his post-September 11th organizational building and rebuilding, Director Mueller was successful in raising FBI performance to new levels through his consistent demand for greater executive accountability and awareness; increased leadership performance; improved attention to detail; sharper mission execution; and clear, complete, and timely investigative reporting. Director Mueller was tough, and he always seemed to be unhappy with whatever was going on—not that he had a lot to be happy about. In addition to his demanding leadership style, the atmosphere around the FBI became one of anxiety and a constant fear of failure as the bureau was being subjected to increasing congressional pressure. Blame had to be assigned and restitution made for what was considered an intelligence failure of the highest order by the FBI.

As part of his strategic realignment of the FBI to keep congressional detractors at bay, Director Mueller's changes in agent hiring priorities in the post-September 11th world deprioritized the recruitment of former law enforcement and military personnel in favor of people with academic backgrounds in fields such as cyber security, political science, and other disciplines that were considered more "intellectual." These new hiring priorities would see the agent workforce change over time. Subsequently, the agent workforce would drift toward different social views and values, thereby causing the FBI to watch its leadership culture change to accommodate a new, but not necessarily better, set of workplace views and values.

While I was still actively involved with field operations and squad-level supervisory duties, and as an ASAC and SAC, I saw instances where some of the newer generations were experiencing challenges in what were previously bedrock special agent activities. For example, some agents who entered into duty under the FBI's revised hiring priorities were struggling with the management of cases and the handling of CHSs (informants). Some of these same agents encountered challenges in establishing command presence when responding to high-stress activities outside of the office environment. I am not sure about any statistical correlation between the FBI's new hiring practices and the emergence of operational challenges, but I personally saw this phenomenon develop on different levels. I heard about it from other FBI managers as well.

As another sign of the times, I saw instances where the newer generations of agents began using email to communicate with and manage their CHSs, which would not provide the relationships required by mission needs. This practice also created records that were not being properly controlled, managed, saved, or stored in private sector channels. I am not sure what FBI CHS handling approach prescribed the general use of non-secure email, but it was not a good trend. Many of the new agents hired under the updated hiring priorities were, in general, very smart, and undoubtedly more capable with the emerging information technology and digital tools. However, I saw this group of agents encounter difficulty with the demands of national security program requirements. This was not their fault, and certainly the FBI could have done a better job in truly mentoring and training them and preparing them for the hazardous and exhausting national security working environment. Without the old breed agents who once trained and conditioned new personnel, I expect that the new agents were largely left to seek out their own mentors and learn how to effectively do their jobs. Several generations of special agents entered into duty during this time that were not provided with the old breed FBI training that I was lucky to have. I remain sorry for that.

I lived through and participated in the FBI's evolution in the post-September 11th world. I saw how Director Mueller's mandated culture change was implemented across the bureau and how it affected the organization. In addition, several resultant organizational factors I witnessed have led the FBI into its current state of leadership and cultural challenges. These factors converged to cause a perceived loss of FBI objectivity and trust with the American people.

The post-September 11th FBI was forced to abruptly abandon its former primary role as a law enforcement agency. This hard shift created confusion due to the forced culture change imposed upon the organization over the next three to five years. In addition to the shockwaves from the rapid pace of organizational recalibration, there was a sense of upheaval and uncertainty as many staff members struggled to understand what was going on. As noted earlier in this book, the bureau was wounded and operating in survival mode, and staff members saw FBIHQ senior leadership becoming overly conciliatory with congressional leaders and other parties of external influence. While it might not have been true in practice, there was a feeling that FBI senior leaders were willing to sacrifice junior personnel to atone for the organization's perceived shortfalls and failures. Staff members also perceived a lack of significant effort on the part of senior leaders to preserve what was still good about the FBI. Among the perceived wreckage, there was much about the FBI that was still good and salvageable; however, much of the pre–September 11th FBI was discarded or left to atrophy to make way for the new FBI.

In addition to the post-September 11th Strategic Execution Team (SET) initiative, Director Mueller's aforementioned changes in FBI hiring priorities would alter the strategic makeup of the special agent cadre for years to come. His newly envisioned special agent population of "digital natives" were seen as being more capable with the new digital resources and communications tools that were being adopted by the FBI (and by its adversaries). The bureau saw its technological IQ improve notably in an investigative sense, and to the lament of many, also in an administrative sense. While people were starting to become more proficient with emerging cyber investigative tools and processes, there was also a proliferation of slideshows and presentations.

As the FBI sought to further corporatize elements of its program management functions, slide decks began to appear everywhere. Inordinate amounts of time and effort were placed on the generation of reports and presentations. New corporate metrics and balanced scorecards began to rule the day. Entire FBIHQ organizational components were created to manage this new administrative industry within the bureau. Field offices had to build entire programs to manage the new corporate HQ demand for business metrics, which took personnel and resources away from core mission investigations. Over time, the collection of metrics and data, along with the delivery of program performance presentations, appeared to become as important as the FBI's core national security and law enforcement missions.

Most of the agents and non-agents who ran these corporate performance metrics machines were products of the new hiring practices favored by Director Mueller and his senior staff (and later expanded by Director Comey and his own staff of metrics and slide deck wizards). While the FBI became increasingly capable in the world of MBA business-speak, these efforts were not directly supporting and enhancing the FBI field operational effort. These "new FBI" corporate metrics managers were seen by many tenured field supervisors and agents as becoming a shadow management structure that had too much direct influence on FBIHQ decision-making and became an indirect parasitic drain on field office resources. Many of these same "new FBI" managers who were highly capable in corporatizing the FBI had little to no familiarity with (or interest in) law enforcement mission principles or field office case management practices. There was also a lack of appreciation for the previously proven leadership principles and practices that once gave the FBI its backbone and steel. (Remember my early mentor "Patton," whose hardcore, effective approach was no longer welcome in the new FBI.) Most of the FBI's historically valued leadership principles were discarded for the new managerial religions of emotional intelligence, servant leadership, corporatized death by metrics, balanced scorecards, and fancy presentations. The people who made up this "new FBI" began moving into various leadership roles. The days of the old-time G-man were finished and were being quickly forgotten.

Eventually, the FBI began taking on a different atmosphere at the senior leadership levels, drifting toward more liberal, private-sector corporate America management perspectives. Emerging FBI leadership approaches included slogans with terms such as transformational, delegative, servant, etc. Unfortunately, these new-age perspectives did not seem to be well-suited to managing the demands of the FBI's multiple threat environments, which required greater mission focus, discipline, execution, and professionalism than our adversaries could muster. To be fair, some of the adopted private sector practices could have been helpful to certain FBI investigative support programs, but any sustainable benefit to the FBI's investigations, operations, and organizational culture remains unclear. Despite the modern private sector's drift toward new leadership approaches that were based more on feelings and personal needs, the FBI's application of these approaches did not make the bureau a better organization. Of course, people enjoyed having a more relaxed work environment after the demanding years of the post-September 11th transition and the stern leadership of Director Mueller; however, discipline across the organization began to erode along with the mission focus that once made the FBI legendary. Along with these shifts in focus, there was a renewed movement to shift special agents out of leadership positions to make room for more non-agent managers—first at FBIHQ and later in field offices. This movement was still in progress when I retired in 2020, with mixed results. It is unclear where the FBI stands at the time of this writing, and it will probably remain unclear as FBI senior leadership continues to put more value into everything looking good instead of everything actually working properly.

The Changing World of the Special Agent

Organizational change across the FBI saw agents being removed from certain managerial positions, with intelligence analysts and non-agent professional support personnel receiving more authority over how the organization operated. As noted earlier, non-agent attorneys were given increased decision-making influence previously reserved for investigative program personnel and this trend continued with other families of non-agent manager roles. Special agent managers and case agents began to feel demoralized in the face of a loss of mission control. In addition, the entire decision-making process was becoming increasingly more centralized with FBIHQ overseeing and driving more of the field office national security operations. Criminal investigative programs remained largely deprioritized by the bureau after September 11th. Criminal programs had been raided for manpower and funding, as a lot of ground had to be made up in properly staffing the growing counterterrorism, counterintelligence, and intelligence programs. In some instances, intelligence analysts began holding positions of authority equal to what was previously held exclusively by agent managers. Under this model, some positions were operated for the better and some were not. A lot of significant structural and cultural change was occurring, and many agents were not ready for those changes. The FBI senior leadership pushed forward. They were either uninformed or indifferent to the strain on the organization, but the systemic cultural change—and erosion—continued.

Shifting Values

With the bureau's changing cultural norms, I saw a corresponding shift in how the newer generations of special agents and intelligence analysts viewed and were oriented to the demands of serving in the FBI. An emerging multi-generational and multi-disciplinary workforce was beginning to question the traditional expectations that had been historically necessary if someone wanted to be part of the organization. For example, this new workforce questioned the long hours and wanted more transparency and direct input for leadership decisions. These and other new workforce demands presented challenges to the more tenured, traditional FBI supervisors in how they managed their programs and staff members. These challenges added new complexity and increased friction. Many tenured managers struggled with how to deal with what was rapidly becoming a multi-cultural and multi-generational FBI. The bureau's approach was to provide training for supervisors in how to accommodate the new human capital challenges in the workplace. I felt that this approach was only a partial solution in that the new hires were not given proper orientation in the bureau's organizational culture and the required practices that were in line with historical FBI norms.

The FBI senior leadership capitulated to the new cultural environment and began to change the organization to accommodate new people, not the other way around, which was a strategic leadership failure.

When I joined the FBI, I knew it was my responsibility to fulfill the bureau's requirements, just as I did in the military. That is what I signed up for. I made adjustments to my own practices meet the FBI's standards and expectations while I dutifully "conducted the director's business." My old breed special agent mentors would not accept anything else. It is what we all did to make sure the FBI remained iconic and successful. I am not sure that this thought process still exists. In fact, I feel that it is now quite the opposite.

Getting Credit

In another example of changing values, I noticed that people began seeking increased recognition and monetary awards for their work. I first noticed this when I was in charge of the Terrorist Screening Center (TSC). As you may recall, the TSC provided twenty-four-hour global watchlisting and screening for terrorist threats and transnational organized crime activities. We were a national security early warning operation formed after September 11, 2001. The center was an essential part of the US government's protective infrastructure, and its excellent staff was certainly deserving of praise and accolades. However, if the TSC did its job properly, no one would even know that it was operating on their behalf.

Over time, some of my TSC staff members began voicing concerns about not receiving recognition from FBIHQ senior leaders, our customers, or the public. I understood, but I would tell them that our chosen job was to quietly maintain the status quo and give people safe places to live and work. Proper TSC mission execution allowed communities of people to travel safely and to live in normalcy, without fear of terrorist attacks. I explained that, in general, no one would come to the center, offer congratulations and accolades, and say, "Hey, great job everyone. Nothing happened today." I also reminded my staff members that the sum of the "thanks" that we will mainly receive is that our combined efforts allowed people to live their lives comfortably and safely in healthy communities, to include our own families and friends. The staff members understood for the most part. The great TSC leadership team consistently recognized the efforts of the staff through formal award programs and informal social recognition, but this change in attitude was new to me. That said, the staff remained true professionals who stood watch twenty-four hours per day in line with the TSC culture to make sure everyone was safe and secure. We just had to learn how to work with some of these new organizational and social dynamics.

There were still many iron men and women at the TSC who worked extremely long and hard to quietly make sure everything was done right and on time—all of the time. I remember having to throw people out of the office to preserve human capital so they would not wear themselves out unnecessarily. But I began to see cracks in the armor of what it once meant to be part of the FBI.

I attributed some of these attitudinal shifts to fatigue on the part of the organization, combined with capitulation to the changes in values and expectations from newer FBI staff members. I also saw that the bureau was no longer willing to hold the line on many traditions in how it conducted its business. So, I began to watch and study these changes to see how we could adapt our leadership approaches in some areas, but hold the line in others, to maintain FBI mission excellence and achievement. But we were in for another wave of change as the FBI's top leadership was about to see a transition. As Director Mueller's extended twelve-year tenure drew to a close in 2013, the FBI was showing signs of burnout, and the bureau was beginning to question its priorities and its future. Enter James B. Comey as the new FBI director.

" The FBI has to do a better job in assessing how it is being perceived. Appearances can make or break the public trust. Earned trust is the most important currency in the FBI's relationship with the American people. How does it regain that trust? "

19

A NEW FBI DIRECTOR AND A NEW WAY OF LOOKING AT THINGS

Director Comey was returning to government service from the private sector. He was pretty much the opposite of Director Mueller in public demeanor and approach. Mueller was stoic, stern, intimidating, and demanding. Comey—even though he was an imposing six feet eight inches tall—immediately proved affable, approachable, and likable to most everyone in the organization. He usually had a smile on his face and was often self-deprecating when talking about his career, his height, and other areas of his life, which put everyone at ease.

Upon his arrival, Comey made a major policy change: he condoned wearing colored dress shirts, ending Mueller's requirement for white dress shirts in business settings. Of course, this was not a major change, but it lightened the general mood. This action, along with Comey's relaxed demeanor, strongly impacted the senior leaders who felt that they could finally exhale and relax after many years of the harsh and unforgiving environment that followed September 11, 2001.

Director Comey took stock of the FBI. I believe he could tell that everyone was exhausted because of the punishing, demanding, zero-defect, survival-based atmosphere that dominated the bureau since September 2001. This atmosphere brooked no failure and allowed for no rest in detecting and defeating acts of global terrorism. While this level of intensity was more than likely required in the prevailing threat environment, Director Comey found FBI people and programs that were fatigued and just limping along. Despite his future challenges, Director Comey's friendlier business approach was welcomed and needed to help the FBI catch its breath and to focus itself for future operations.

Evolution or Devolution

While some relief in the intensity of operations was helpful to the health and sanity of the staff, the more relaxed environment eventually drifted too far, and the bureau began losing its edge in some areas. Some of the mission attributes that made the FBI effective in the post-September 11th threat environment began to fade in certain areas, while some were pretty much deprioritized. Everything across the FBI became negotiable and up for questioning. Gone were the days of military precision and bearing in presentations for Director Mueller. We no longer had to fear the potential for director-level cross-examinations on case briefs to keep discipline strong. The sharp execution and ultra-accountability that Mueller demanded were eased. It was not that Director Comey was receptive to mediocrity, but he was much more congenial and more understanding about small mistakes, so people were no longer horrified about making them. The only problem was that the acceptance of small mistakes led to laxity, and then laxity resulted in lower performance and declines in discipline over time.

A New FBI Director and a New Way of Looking at Things

As noted earlier, many organizational practices that were previously non-negotiable became open for debate and occasional disregard. For example, from a chain-of-command perspective, virtually no one from the FBI rank and file would have dared to directly contact Director Mueller, the deputy director, or other senior FBI executives to voice grievances. In contrast, Director Comey welcomed direct communications from the workforce, and many people (probably too many) took him up on this accommodation. Direct communication between Director Comey and the workforce (and, by extension, the deputy director) eventually created an atmosphere of sub-surface chaos and accelerated a decline in discipline. As an added distraction from daily operations, FBI leaders had to jump through hoops to answer questions from the director and deputy director in response to workforce grievances that should have been resolved at the lowest echelons. Supervisors now had to cover their asses and be ready at the proverbial "drop of a hat" to explain how they were dealing with dissatisfied staff members, managing personnel issues, and pursuing real or perceived program challenges.

The integrity of the chain of command continued to decline under the new FBI organizational dynamics that empowered people to freely complain, air grievances, or tattle on coworkers. Discipline further eroded, and the organizational attribute of stoically and patiently working through problems also faded. The staff became impatient in using their chains of command to resolve problems and to get work done. They no longer felt compelled to work through issues with their immediate supervisors since they could now engage personally with the director or deputy director. While some people hailed these developments as improvements in transparency and communication, it seemed that we were approaching a state where too much of a good thing was no longer a good thing.

With this new era of bureau leadership, we also saw that complaining (and sometimes outright whining) was being tolerated as a means of encouraging "transparency." While I believe that staff members should be heard, they should not expect to be catered to just because they shared their ideas (or made the ever-helpful anonymous complaint). Over time, despite what some of my former colleagues may argue, people's feelings began to carry equal or sometimes even higher priority than core mission effectiveness and operational execution. It appeared that keeping people happy was taking top billing with many supervisors to gain favor with the FBI senior leadership and garner promotion favorability. This was not the fault of the intermediate or line supervisory personnel but, rather, the direct responsibility of the director, deputy director, and other sympathetic senior leaders. They chose to create a new leadership environment where being liked took on a tangible value for FBI leaders.

While moving into its new strategic and leadership approaches, FBI senior leadership became distracted by trying to be more like private sector America (Google, Netflix, JP Morgan, etc.). The bureau also became interested in diversity matters (before the advent of current diversity, equity, and inclusion trends). It became fixated on selecting leaders who were popular, and the selection process focused on workplace climate surveys and candidate diversity as opposed to leadership attributes such as leadership maturity, operational achievement, and business acumen. Instead of becoming the leadership factory that Director Comey envisioned, the FBI began producing groups of timid yet likable leaders who seemed overly concerned with special emphases on cultural programs, corporate metrics, and risk scores. These organizational factors were much easier to deal with than the tough, sometimes unpopular business of maintaining excellence and achievement in leadership practices and investigative operations (as in the Olympic athlete abuse case).

All of this change occurred when the FBI had a growing need for capable leaders who could make difficult decisions, solve problems, move the mission forward, maintain standards, and swiftly resolve any personnel issues professionally and objectively. What the FBI received instead was a leadership environment that prioritized being easy-going and well-liked. The FBI grew leaders who became more interested in baby showers, birthday parties, and bowling retreats. As FBI leaders became more risk-averse and concerned about "likability," some leaders and staff members started looking for safer ways to move through their careers. I remember this old saying in the FBI: "Big cases, big problems; small cases, small problems; no cases, no problems." While this saying used to be jokingly said among supervisors and case agents, risk averseness and organizational timidity became more of a reality and hindrances to FBI mission effectiveness over time.

Introducing a Culture of Trepidation

I have mentioned the use (and misuse) of climate surveys, and you can probably tell that I was not a proponent of this tool. The surveys became an annual distraction that lasted for several months in the spring of each year. It became a running joke that no tough decisions or performance problems would be addressed from November through March because those in charge did not want staff payback on their climate surveys. I saw these climate surveys as a primary cause (or maybe an accelerator) of the supervisory timidity that steadily eroded the bureau's bravery, toughness, and effectiveness.

The FBI expanded the broad use of climate surveys circa the 2008 timeframe to assess the organizational environment in such areas as leadership, staff member contentment, and mission connection. While the surveys were used during the time of Director Mueller, their use was further formalized with Director Comey. Director Mueller used to joke that he always got bad climate surveys (when he made a joke once or twice a year), but he did not perseverate on survey scores. Director Comey made the survey scores a primary assessment tool, and Deputy Director McCabe (and his successor) further heightened the impact of survey scores by requiring their use in performance appraisals and inclusion in promotion packages.

During my career as an FBI manager, I saw instances where highly effective program supervisors received less than stellar climate survey results in the "people skills" areas. These lower survey scores mainly occurred because the supervisors did not tolerate laziness, nonsense, immaturity, or low performance in their programs. In the programs that I oversaw, the managers who received lower "people skill" scores were professionals who had high expectations and demanded accountability and results. I also knew some of the staff members whom they supervised, and I could generally recognize childish behavior in what amounted to climate survey counterpunching. As a result, these highly capable supervisors would get lower than expected scores in certain rating areas that I took in stride given the circumstances. I took a more passive approach to climate surveys unless I could tell that an actual problem had developed and required corrective action, but I could often identify such areas early on and apply corrections before climate survey season. Every year, I talked with the supervisors about their scores, and I would give and receive feedback. I made it a practice to never chastise supervisors based solely on survey results without other supporting information—positive or negative. Chastising only led to people becoming defensive where they no longer listened but, instead, focused on resisting critique and justifying their positions. Instead, I casually stressed the importance of good business practices, professionalism, and consistency over chasing staff approval and seeking favorable scores. I would also restate my expectations for how the staff was to be treated—with professionalism, dignity, and common courtesy at a minimum. As there was no blame present, I rarely had anyone become irate over the climate survey results. In my eyes, the climate survey was a diagnostic tool and was not to be used to damage careers. I never let that happen to members of my leadership teams.

While I was not in favor of using the climate surveys to significantly impact careers, I was in the minority among managers, as many sought to match Director Comey's leaning toward private sector management principles. As such, the FBI saw a marked increase in the use of climate survey results for career progression and promotion. At one point, the results were inserted into senior executive service reviews (possibly impacting end-of-year monetary bonuses). Intermediate managers were also subject to the results being used as evaluation criteria in their promotion selections.

Over time, senior and intermediate leaders became more concerned about how they led and managed to avoid scrutiny and minimize impact to their promotion potential. In some instances, this increased concern resulted in improved managerial performance, but I saw more detriment than benefit. Some managers became aloof, while others began coddling their staff members and chasing higher climate survey scores to enhance their promotion potential. All managers began looking for "dark green", which was a visual-aid color scheme showing the highest band of favorable scores. I did not clearly see how the surveys helped leaders professionally manage investigative personnel, programs, systems, and resources in defeating national security threats and crime problems. The FBI might have become a more congenial and employee-friendly place to work, but I came to believe that the climate surveys probably hurt more than they helped. We will probably never know what the impact was, is, or will be to the boldness, initiative, and guts of field agents and the general supervisory cadre.

As an example of the FBI's cultural erosion and the increased timidity of its personnel, I recall a situation that still has me shaking my head. I attended an off-site event in Washington, DC. It was close to the WFO, so I parked the vehicle I was using there and walked to the event venue. When I was departing the event, I noticed a few FBI folks huddled around an older gentleman. I stopped and saw former FBI Director William H. Webster in the center of the group. As I questioned the agents about what was going on, I noticed that one of them appeared to be harried as they were frantically trying to find the former director a ride to his DC office. When I asked why one of the agents was not giving Director Webster a ride, they said they were not allowed to do so. I then asked what the problem was. They responded that they had talked to OGC, and an attorney there said that a ride for the former director was not authorized. I was stunned. The fact that they asked permission signaled that these were not old breed special agents, nor were they the product of old breed training and mentoring. The old breed would have given the former director a ride because it was the right and proper thing to do, even if not immediately approved. Explanations could have been provided later, if necessary.

I thought that the agents standing with former Director Webster meant well in trying to arrange for a taxi, but I was

A New FBI Director and a New Way of Looking at Things

concerned that they were all too afraid of getting into trouble by giving him a ride across town. Former Director Webster was a gentleman at an advanced age (maybe in his mid-nineties at the time), and he was becoming confused and uncomfortable. I told the agents that I would give former Director Webster a ride to his office across town. I asked them to stay with him while I walked to get my vehicle. I picked Director Webster up from the side of the street and safely brought him to his office without incident. There were no problems, and there was no purposeful impropriety to fret about with the lawyers.

This situation was disappointing all around. I saw timid agents who were afraid to do the right thing because of a misguided interpretation of a general administrative rule. I also saw excessive agent deference to the word of attorneys who could offer legal opinions but had no supervisory authority. I witnessed fear of getting into trouble as the primary cause of an absence of common courtesy for the former director. What happened to my FBI?

The bottom line is that the agents were scared to get into trouble, which created a lack of common sense and indicated that a culture of ass-covering was becoming more prevalent in the FBI. But I do not blame the personnel who were involved; this was a leadership problem. Fear became rampant to the point where those in leadership positions were reluctant to make hard or unpopular (but right) decisions that might violate a ridiculous administrative rule. FBI personnel should be able to depend on their senior leaders to protect them from administrative chickenshit when they are doing the right things for the right reasons. **How can we expect FBI special agents to make hard decisions, do dangerous things, go to dangerous places, and engage with dangerous people on our behalf when the organization has beaten them into**

submission over low-value administrative matters? This situation was disappointing evidence that the people of the FBI had been effectively sedated by the threat of getting into trouble or by hurting their future chances for promotion. The bureau had firmly moved into a place of "going along to get along" instead of taking the hard, right path that might not be in line with certain administrative policies.

I saw this situation as an example of the impact of the chickenshit mentality that had infiltrated and polluted the FBI over time. For reference in what "chickenshit" entails, I will offer this excellent definition from a military perspective (substitute FBI context where applicable):

> Chickenshit refers to behavior that makes military life worse than it need be: petty harassment of the weak by the strong; open scrimmage for power and authority and prestige ... and insistence on the letter rather than the spirit of the ordinances. Chickenshit is so called—instead of horse- or bull- or elephant-shit—because it is small-minded and ignoble and takes the trivial seriously. Chickenshit can be recognized instantly because it never has anything to do with winning the war. (Paul Fussell, *Wartime: Understanding and Behavior in the Second World War*, 1989)

Social Perception and Appearances

In contrast to the dominance of internal chickenshit, the social perception of the FBI by the communities it serves is another area in which I have seen some questionable practices. Since my retirement in 2020, I have heard anecdotal accounts and have seen media coverage of heavy-handed FBI approaches in dealing with people who held political views that were reportedly not in favor with the current power structure.

A New FBI Director and a New Way of Looking at Things

FBI searches of the residences of prominent political figures were seen by the public as being excessive and possibly politically motivated. There have also been reports of investigative overkill for the pursuit of certain political event participants. I have seen videos and still photos of agents outfitted with paramilitary gear and military-style rifles, which is not the image most people hold of FBI special agents.

FBI special agents kneeling at Lafayette Park during the Black Lives Matter (aka BLM) marches in Washington, DC, circa June 2020, comes to mind when considering social perceptions. I was floored by this weak, conciliatory action, and I wanted to know who was in charge at the scene. I had recently retired when this event occurred, and every time I saw photos from this regrettable event, my heart broke. The FBI that I once knew did not kneel for anyone and did not show open deference for specific social causes. Such overt displays of social deference could indicate bias and must be strongly discouraged by leaders as the bureau works to repair and maintain its perceived objectivity and apolitical stance. I am confident that the old breed special agents I trained under would not have approved of the actions taken at Lafayette Park that day. We would have had our tails kicked for doing something like that. Instead, the Lafayette Park kneeling agents were reportedly given coffee shop gift cards. I am not sure what has happened to the FBI, but it must immediately marshal its people and resources to recover the warriorship, stoic professionalism, and principled leadership that will be required to recover the organization's soul.

Operational Appearances

I recall that, during the early part of my career, most FBI operations were professional, well-planned, low-key, and whenever possible, non-confrontational. Aside from the occasional planned "perp walk," a practice that was eventually discouraged, I saw no media photo opportunities when agents made an arrest. Unlike some current operations, the news media was not routinely on site to film agents in military gear with rifles. These recently adopted practices were not consistent with previous tactics, which were normally executed without excessive weaponry, fanfare, and media coverage. Of course, agent and officer safety in field operations should be of the highest priority and a primary component of operational planning and I believe that agents should be provided with the best protective gear to keep them safe while they execute their duties. I am just not sure that most operations require military gear, garb, and weapons for personnel who do not serve in a dedicated tactical or high-risk role (e.g., SWAT operators, fugitive task force members, or violent crime program investigators). I have seen a drift in media-covered FBI operations that tends to take on a more military or tactical image, and I am not sure the FBI should strive for this. Does this image promote tactical capability? Sure. But does it help the bureau relate to the society it serves? No—not in my view. Personally, I prefer a professional, conservative suit (minus the fedora of the old breed) from a time when appearance and attitude were a major part of the FBI brand. This brand was required, and agents were expected to look a certain way and to behave in a professional, dignified manner at all times (no kneeling allowed).

Early in my career, I supported an operation in which our Newark Field Office violent crime squad would be arresting members of the Outlaw Motorcycle Gang. To prepare for this operation, all non-SWAT agents carried service pistols, along with any miscellaneous gear they needed.

As an aside, I remembered my time in the Prince Street Projects in Newark, New Jersey, when we were taught to stay light and mobile. For this arrest operation, we had old-style bulletproof vests (the white and blue reversible models), and I think there were a few FBI baseball caps and some of those old garbage bag-looking FBI windbreaker raid jackets in use. But that was it.

When setting up for the motorcycle gang arrest, a number of bureau cars were strategically set up on a few streets around the Outlaw clubhouse, and we waited until our SWAT team entered and cleared the place of immediate threats. Fortunately, no shots were fired, and no other unfavorable incidents were reported upon SWAT entry. After the SWAT team secured the site, they fell back to their tactical vehicle and departed. Then all of the agents on scene facilitated site security, evidence collection, and arrestee processing.

We brought all the Outlaw members out of the clubhouse and sat them on a curb while they waited to be processed. While standing with this group, I noticed that most of the members were older gentlemen, but they all wore their Outlaw colors. I also saw some younger men with "one percenter" identification patches and all of the other markings that indicated that they were dangerous people.

We were standing and talking with them, and one of them said something along the lines of "Oh yeah, we knew you guys were the Feds."

We looked at him and asked, "What do you mean?"

The guy who made the initial comment said, "Yeah, you guys look like Feds, and you weren't assholes. You guys treated us like ... people, you know?"

Even these Outlaw gang members expected "the Feds" to be professional—and that's what they got. No excessive military gear or weapons were needed after the SWAT team cleared the clubhouse. There was no yelling, and no rifles were carried openly. No news crews were standing around taking video and pictures (smart phones and social media did not exist at the time). It was just a safe arrest operation that was well-planned, well-staffed, and well-executed. There was no fanfare, and the community was a safer place afterward. Absent a few special circumstances that required a more tactical approach, this is how FBI business was usually done.

Certain recent appearances have not been exactly favorable to the FBI. On some occasions, the news media has reported FBI surveillance activities that reportedly skirted the edges of First Amendment-protected activities at schools and school board meetings. We have also seen reports of confrontations with American citizens who oppose certain prevailing political ideologies or who hold beliefs that have fallen out of vogue with the current government administration. Social media footage has shown people identified as FBI agents appearing at private homes to ask questions about certain social media activities. FISA Section 702 surveillance privacy issues have also raised alarms about how the government can collect information on US citizens without warrants (which is not really true, but no one is interested in the facts). Some situations might be explainable or even unavoidable; however, the bureau rarely looks good when such situations occur. While many of these situations and unflattering circumstances may not be as they are cast, FBI leadership must take stock of how they appear to the American people. I know how these operations are supposed to work, but the vast majority of Americans do not. There is an old saying about perception being reality. The FBI has to do a better job in assessing how it is being perceived. Appearances can make or break the public trust. Earned trust is the most important currency in the FBI's relationship with the American people. How does it regain that trust?

SECTION III

MOVING THE FBI FORWARD: RESTORING FAITH

> "When I was leading FBI people and programs, I believed that everything we did should be excellent and that we should set the standard for every practice or discipline."

20

HOW DOES THE FBI MOVE AHEAD?

Now that we have discussed the FBI's challenges, we will consider how the organization can do better—and do so right away. It can start on the road to recovery by swallowing its pride and admitting that it is not what it can or should be. It should realign itself with its legacy and its relationship with the American people. Of course, the FBI does not have the time or luxury of sitting and licking its wounds while the world becomes more dangerous and complex. But I believe the FBI can change quickly without severely interrupting its operations, once again making excellence its highest priority.

The New Rules to Live By

When I was leading FBI people and programs, I believed that everything we did should be excellent and that we should set the standard for every practice or discipline. What can be so hard about that in principle? I used to tell my staff members that we did important and hard things. If our tasks and objectives were easy, then someone else would have already done them. I always felt that the FBI had to take pride in the fact that it was expected to take on difficult, complex, or dangerous tasks that others could not or would not do. I began hearing too much talk about circumstances being difficult as

I moved through my career. I am not sure why that kind of talk became more common around the organization—maybe it was those multi-generational attitude changes I spoke about earlier. Maybe organizational fatigue. Maybe a lack of organizational steel and toughness. Maybe a lack of stoic, principled leadership. Maybe all of these things.

During my last and most senior FBI leadership position, I used a large white board in my office for messaging and for the overt display of preferred operating principles that people could easily see, I listed these operating principles that characterized how we were expected to do hard things, be excellent in conducting FBI business, and offer no complaint. The list below includes supporting language that was based on numerous conversations with my team. These became known as the Rules to Live By:

1. **Tough shit:** Tasks in our line of work can be challenging. Heavy lifting is what the FBI does. When something goes bad, we work harder and find solutions. We lead, and we do not buckle or give in. People depend on us to manage hard things and solve tough problems better than anyone else, without reservation or complaint.
2. **If it does not suck, we do not do it:** If problems were easily and readily manageable or resolvable, someone else would have already handled them. The FBI routinely deals with the complex and the dangerous. We seek out what sucks so we can sharpen our superior skills to do what others cannot or will not do. When people are scared or in danger and things really suck, they should always know that the FBI is their best bet.
3. **Assumption is the cause of bad outcomes:** We should refrain from assumption whenever possible.

On the easy side of the consequence scale, assumption can be the cause of missed deadlines, incomplete work, or a lack of achievement. On the hard side of this scale, assumption can lead to mission failure, property damage, injury, or loss of life. We strive for mission success by testing and verifying expected outcomes—we do not assume.

4. **Never be a liability:** We will always strive to provide value in everything we do, whether the FBI is leading or supporting. When leading, our work will be exceptional, and we will be considerate of what must be done and by whom. When supporting, we will be respectful and always looking for ways to help. We want to be a resource, no matter what is going on. We will be enthusiastic, resilient, and open-minded. When in charge, we will pull. When supporting, we will push. We will be an asset at all times.

By instilling these four principles across all program activities, the FBI would again become unmatched and unbeatable. These principles can foster a winning mindset, build more beneficial operational practices, and fuel an organizational recovery. After these principles are modeled by FBI leaders and fully integrated into the bureau's organizational culture, assertive execution should be prioritized into simple action plans that everyone can understand and reference. From an organizational perspective, the following points are provided as macro principles that the FBI (or any struggling organization) can adopt and execute to begin a recovery without overly impairing or impacting operations.

Ten Principles for Rebuilding the FBI

FBI leadership could make a significant impact by creating objectives that will be applied to all people and programs managed by the FBI—without fail or compromise. A true return to excellence will leave no ambiguity in its objectives and will tolerate no adversarial or undermining behaviors. To show the way forward, a summary set of principles and objectives can serve as a guide and should be written down and made readily available for reference across the organization. Then people can see leadership intent, know where the organization is heading, and decide if they want to stay and help rebuild. They will also be able to determine if they cannot align themselves with the updated principles and practices. There should be no surprises. If people cannot or will not align themselves with the stated way forward, an amicable parting of ways might be best for all parties.

I. Cultural Reinforcement and Realignment

The FBI senior leadership infrastructure must be immediately overhauled and must emphasize earnest demonstrations of the following foundational principles:

- Principled leadership
- Selfless service
- Ethical objectivity
- Intellectual honesty
- Dedication to mission focus and excellence
- Sound judgment

These basic concepts must be adopted throughout the organization. Working for the FBI cannot be merely a "job," because its mission is too important for so many people. The current bureau culture must be recalibrated to reinvigorate and reinforce the dedication that was historically embodied by FBI service. The principles provided immediately above will serve as the umbrella under which the rebuilding can be successfully accomplished. All leadership, from the director to the line supervisors, must nurture these principles as the foundation of the FBI's organizational traits and culture. Senior leadership must then lead by example. If the bureau succumbs to a defective or irrelevant culture, the introduction of new technology, training courses, or other managerial eyewash will make no difference. Forcing good people to work in a bad culture will almost always see the bad culture come out on top—and everyone loses. Fix the culture and find action-oriented, principled leaders who will live by the foundational principles. This is where true change starts.

II. Leadership Development and Strategic Planning

The FBI must reestablish a leadership environment that demonstrates the fidelity, bravery, and integrity that the organization espouses. Leadership cannot be formed around the latest slogan or a collection of leadership buzz terms that no one puts into practice. All leaders—from the director to first-line supervisors—must rededicate themselves to working responsibly on behalf of the American people. The world is becoming more dangerous, and there is no time for personal agendas, political leanings, or ego-driven decision-making. Avoid happy talk, leadership lectures, and book reading lists, as these cosmetic fixes will not change the fabric of the organization. Senior leaders must objectively reward the behaviors that exemplify the organization's core values. The FBI must discourage boat anchors such as excessive egos, careerism, cowardice, parochialism, pettiness, laziness, and excessive personal interest. Priority must be placed on implementing a leadership development program that not only prepares individuals for their roles but also consistently focuses on modeling behaviors that project mission excellence. The FBI must also emphasize operational success by aligning leadership practices with strategic objectives rather than making abrupt changes that can occur during every new leadership transition. Whenever possible, strategic leadership plans should be projected approximately eighteen to twenty-four months and should clearly map out activities, resources, and objectives. The bureau must reset its attitude toward the use of organizational metrics as FBI leadership often confuses strategic and tactical planning. Many managers also confuse measurements of activity with actual performance in assessing organizational accomplishment. Future leadership models must offer a clear approach to set all of these factors into proper contexts. After establishing the desired expectations and organizational practices, leadership by example and having strategic vision will be keys to success.

III. Reorient/Rebuild the Mid-Level Leadership Cadre

The FBI must reassess its mid-level management cadre (GS 14 and GS 15) to ensure that the right people with the right experience and attributes are in the right roles. As these people form the pool from which most of the organization's eventual senior leaders are drawn, the bureau must carefully select and train this level of managers to be principled leaders, make informed decisions in line with mission objectives, and exemplify FBI cultural norms. All too often, I have seen people get promoted as a reward for longevity, to avoid lawsuits, or to quickly fill a vacant position. These shortsighted leadership selections have rarely, if ever, benefited the FBI and its people in the long run. As such, FBI senior leaders must put more time, interest, and resources into training and mentoring their successors. To minimize instances of groupthink and going along to get along, FBI mid-level leaders should be trained and encouraged to present alternate opinions and courses of action with professional candor without fear of reprisal. That said, once a lawful decision has been made, mid-level managers must execute the mission to the best of their ability. Mid-level leaders must understand that professional candor and mission focus will be essential in facilitating the FBI's organizational recovery efforts. The FBI has to create several waves of old breed special agents and professional support personnel who will make sure that their future managers are doing what is right and keeping things right—the FBI way.

IV. Rebuilding and Reassessing Priorities

While diversity, equity, and inclusion are important factors in organizational dynamics, the FBI must ensure that it returns its primary organizational focus to promoting professionalism, discipline, investigative objectivity, and operational excellence. Organizational development initiatives and special cultural emphasis programs must complement the bureau's core mission rather than overshadow or distract from it. There should be no need for special programs to ensure that FBI leaders and program managers treat everyone with dignity and courtesy. FBI leaders, as part of regular practice, should be expected to provide equitable support for staff development and professional opportunities. These practices should be a standing part of the FBI's organizational culture. The FBI must rebalance its approach to developing its personnel while emphasizing the integration of leadership, human capital, and technology that will be necessary to combat future national security threats and crime problems.

V. Accountability and Integrity

The FBI must once again foster cultural accountability and integrity as top priorities. The bureau has to encourage all leaders and staff members to take ownership of their decisions and actions, including acknowledging and learning from mistakes. General accountability has often been eroded by zero-defect program management approaches that are defective in their own right as human beings are not capable of operating without mistakes or misunderstandings. Zero defect approaches destroy accountability due to fear of blanket reprisal or punishment. Accountability can have many meanings, but the simple definition I have always had success with is "doing what you are supposed to be doing and doing what you say you are doing." Very simple. In order to move forward, FBI leaders must provide an environment of accountability in which people are willing to solve problems without fear of unearned reprisal. Establishing such an environment would be essential to turning the organization around and giving people ownership in their successes and in resolving any shortfalls. Integrity is one of the bureau's primary espoused values and must be reprioritized in how people execute their duties. Integrity is simply doing the right thing at the right time for the right reasons—especially when no one is watching. If the FBI cannot retool its application of accountability and integrity, then the organization is lost.

VI. Training and Development

Training of agents and professional support personnel, particularly in areas critical to the organization's investigative mission, should include topics surrounding advanced investigative techniques, operational execution, organizational management, business acumen, problem-solving, and complex threat resolution. The FBI must return to the competence and excellence that previously set it apart from other government agencies. The bureau's Training Division and FBI Academy must update their training philosophies to provide real-world skill sets that advance the mission. For special agent personnel, recurrent skill training has not been consistent and cannot be properly provided through online digital training formats. Watching instructional videos can be sufficient for basic orientation on foundational concepts, but only qualified, experienced instructors can teach people how to apply training concepts to real-world situations. This approach can be time-consuming in that it requires exposure to scenarios and responses to simulated threats in applicable environments and will require leadership sponsorship and support. An example of specialized training could be the recruitment of CHSs (informants). Learning to handle CHSs against sophisticated organized crime and international criminal elements requires targeted training and mentorship. Competing against sophisticated nation-state adversaries, hostile intelligence services, and international criminal organizations that seek to defeat the United States requires more intense training than most people have received from the FBI. Attempts have been made in the past to provide such training, but many beneficial courses were not adequately staffed, updated, or sustained. Training will not necessarily be the answer to all of the FBI's problems, but it can be a useful tool in providing skills and building perspectives needed by FBI personnel on all levels to avoid operational hazards, make good decisions, and effectively solve problems.

VII. Planning and Metrics

The FBI can benefit from developing strategic plans that maintain consistent direction in core objectives and priority program activities. In addition, tactical leadership changes and programmatic adaptations must not lead to drastic shifts in strategic focus but instead build on past successes. Periodic changes in bureau leadership have historically resulted in wholesale changes to entire programs without articulating new operational requirements, required tactical shifts, or strategic alignment with FBI corporate priorities. Such changes are often personality-based and have resulted in wasted resources, funding challenges, high staff fatigue, and low staff morale. When assuming a strategic view of FBI operations, leadership must focus on organizational alignment and avoid the over-metrication of operations that can prioritize short-term administrative primacy over short- and long-term operational excellence. All leaders and program managers must resist dwelling on immediate details and invasive metrics that can hinder creativity and paralyze the organization. Just because something can be measured does not necessarily mean that it must be.

VIII. Transparency and Communication

The FBI can improve communication throughout the organization as well as with national leaders, partners, and the public. The bureau has to remove the fabled government "information stovepipes" (overt and covert) and encourage the sharing of information in integrated program collaborations. Leaders and program managers must provide regular information updates, guidance documents, and cultural reinforcements to manage expectations and outcomes. Wherever possible, the FBI should offer open dialogues about operational and organizational challenges with internal and external stakeholders to help rebuild confidence. I am not talking about oversharing investigative information, which can cause a reduction in operational effectiveness—common sense should be the rule. Encourage sharing that is desired and preclude what is unwanted by creating inclusive relationships, goals, objectives, and incentives. Make sure everyone understands leadership intent, as communication is not an exact science. Communication is an infinite process and leaders are never "done" with this key part of human interaction.

IX. Rebuilding Brand and Reputation

The FBI must focus on rebuilding its brand and its standing with the national leadership and the American people. This requires possibly redefining why the bureau exists, what its purpose is, and how it conducts its business. The FBI must focus on what it does and not as much on what it says. As noted earlier, happy talk, eyewash, and outright bullshit may be sufficient to quell congressional inquiries or respond to OIG findings, but real change will require action over words. The FBI must launch a comprehensive outreach effort to rebuild its reputation with **all** of its stakeholders. Being honest, admitting mistakes, and addressing past shortcomings must be sincere and earnest to garner any benefit. Otherwise, we will only see another round of talk that will waste everyone's time. The FBI brand—fidelity, bravery, and integrity—should be meaningful, demonstrable, and bankable.

X. Stakeholder Engagement

The FBI must reset its engagement with stakeholders, including Congress, to address concerns, clarify its role, and demonstrate a renewed commitment to balanced relationships to help alleviate scrutiny and skepticism. Proper recalibration and a restoration of trust in the FBI will be necessary to prevent the appearance of improper relationships with private entities. The bureau must interact regularly with stakeholders to fuel dialogues and establish beneficial relationships during good times, as opposed to showing up only when something is wrong or in the execution of a law enforcement action.

Embracing and Sustaining Change

Rebuilding the FBI's culture, reputation, and effectiveness could be a complex endeavor; however, this action can be executed relatively quickly by those who still believe in its mission. Commitment will be required from leadership, staff, and stakeholders without distraction. While the FBI can quickly make many short-term operational changes, some elements of change cannot happen within the usual 90- to 180-day work cycles and will require fundamental organizational realignments. For example, the right (or suitable) senior leadership team will have to be formed to restore the bureau's alignment with its core mission set. These leaders will have to act boldly and will also have to exemplify the desired behaviors and practices that the staff, our country's leadership, and the American people deserve. Only then can the FBI begin moving assertively toward regaining its legendary status as a trustworthy, dependable, effective US institution.

The FBI must change to once again become one of this nation's primary points of stability, justice, and trust. The bureau is no stranger to change, but it must accept and manage change, as opposed to avoiding or just reacting to it. The following excerpt was said by the first and founding FBI director, and it should be a primary consideration for every director to follow:

> Today ... the FBI is in the midst of great change—operationally, organizationally, administratively. A direct response to the critical needs of our nation. There's no doubt that this transformation will be successful. The bureau has a long history of changing

and evolving in order to meet the needs of the American people. (J. Edgar Hoover, director, Federal Bureau of Investigation [1924 - 1972])

The hope is that the FBI will make the necessary changes to its culture, leadership, and practices and find its way back to serving the needs of the American people; however, we all know that hope is not a plan or a solution.

"Can the FBI recover from its troubles and regain its proud standing with the American people?"

21

CLOSING THOUGHTS

The Federal Bureau of Investigation of the United States Department of Justice. The FBI. This is still one of the most well-known acronyms around the world; however, some of the luster and shine associated with this storied organization may have dimmed. For some thoughts on why this might have happened, I offered personal perspectives and my experiences and looked at the organization's journey (as well as my own) after the events on September 11, 2001.

During my time with the bureau, I was fortunate to be trained under old breed special agents who were protectors of the FBI faith. They passed their ethics and insights to me and others, as they eventually had to leave the organization behind. In their honor, I wrote this book to preserve some of their lessons and ideas. I also sought to reveal some of the factors that may have impacted the FBI in the areas of leadership, organizational culture, and mission clarity over the course of my twenty-five-year career. Some of my experiences, from street agent to executive assistant director, were provided to start an honest discussion about how the bureau could overcome its current challenges and return to its previous positions of trust and confidence with the American people.

This book also presented a cautionary tale of how the FBI, known as a high-performing, storied organization, could fall victim to the corporate diseases of cultural erosion, leadership atrophy, complacency, and distraction from the core mission. Many of the challenges discussed in this book could be easily applied to other organizations that are struggling. If these challenges can happen to an elite organization like the FBI, then they can happen (and have happened) to just about any organization.

Can the FBI recover from its troubles and regain its proud standing with the American people? It will be a challenging task. However, I believe that, with principled leadership, the FBI can quickly recover if it is willing to uncompromisingly implement the recommendations offered in this book and make difficult but appropriate personnel changes. The FBI has to take a critical look at itself and, with a profound sense of organizational humility, reconnect with its core values, and refocus its mission priorities. The FBI must reestablish the unquestionable character, common sense, and unbreakable backbone that once defined the organization.

Fostering a Climate of Honesty

While the FBI may have become somewhat distracted over time by politics, social trends, and internal ideological shifts, I still believe that it can once again skillfully navigate the Washington, DC, minefield in service to our complex society. It can do this by reconstituting its character so it can be fully entrusted with the apolitical enforcement of our nation's laws. The FBI must once again be without reproach in its objectivity to transcend political influences. The bureau must do everything with the highest levels of competence and integrity to restore confidence across our country's political sector. The FBI also has work to do in restoring its image and standing with the American public. A sense of doubt seems prevalent in the minds of the American people. According to a recent poll, the FBI had an approximate 10 percent approval rating (Mood of the Nation Poll, McCourtney Institute for Democracy, November 2022). This is unacceptable, and the bureau should remember that the American people grant the trust that allows it to operate on behalf of the people. In the words of the great Benjamin Franklin, "Honesty is the best policy," and the preservation of such honesty is where the fidelity, bravery, and integrity that the FBI was known for should shine brightest.

A Mandate for Strong Executive Leadership

As discussed earlier, the FBI's director and their executive leadership team are the primary protectors of the FBI brand. These leaders, the strategic heads of the organization, have to elevate the bureau above the political fray. These leaders must support and enable the special agents who regularly visit the social and political swamps of society to do what the FBI does best: objectively and skillfully conduct investigations and professionally enforce the laws of our nation. The FBI director and his executive leadership team should be capable of guiding the organization, so it keeps pace with current and emerging threats while it balances its operations with the needs of the American people. These senior executives must be trusted do the right thing—no matter what—in the eyes of our national leaders and the American public. FBI executive leaders should exemplify how to skillfully make hard decisions, be objective in their judgment, make good business decisions, and speak with professional candor regardless of outcomes. These behaviors also have to be modeled for the rest of the organization. The FBI senior executives of the future cannot be seen as political operatives or as individuals who can be easily swayed by partisan political pressure, fleeting public opinion, or the mob mentality of social media. The FBI director and his executive leaders have to collectively be the bellwether that the rest of the bureau, as well as the law enforcement community, can follow.

The deputy director is the second in charge of the FBI and the chief operational figure in the organization. This person must have the same attributes and character traits as the director because the executive heads of all fifty-six field offices report directly to him (or her). This role steers the cultural and strategic directions that influence the field office operations of the FBI. Future deputy directors and heads of field offices must model the fidelity, bravery, and integrity that are expected from the rest of the rank and file. These leaders also must inspire with candor and demand operational excellence while they treat people with dignity and courtesy. When the bureau drifts off course, it is the job of the deputy director to make it right. When the organization is struggling, the deputy director's responsibility is to gather their executive leaders, marshal applicable personnel and resources, and collaboratively resolve challenges that affect our communities and national interests. The deputy director should be the organizational champion for the concepts in the "New Rules to Live By" provided earlier. An assertive implementation of these principles by all levels of the organization would make the FBI unbeatable and feared once again by hostile nation-state adversaries and criminals from all walks of life.

The selection of the future FBI director, deputy director, and their executive leaders must prioritize the rebuilding of leadership principles and practices for the FBI. If need be, a wholesale turnover in the FBI's senior leader ranks must be considered to secure the right people for the right roles for the right reason. The American people can no longer suffer inconsistencies in the fidelity, bravery, and integrity that the FBI requires to ensure the future existence of our way life. In addition, the entire bureau leadership cadre must once again treat leadership as a privilege and ensure that only the best leaders have the opportunity to work for the American people.

Mission Clarity and Reconnection

To sustain the required mission clarity and connection, the FBI should continually define how it will consistently fulfill its mission to "protect the American people and uphold the Constitution." This process of mission definition cannot be seen as a finite activity, and there can be no finish line or completion date. The FBI should remain in a dynamic cycle of self-assessment as it combats evolving national security threats and emerging crime problems. Rebuild the organization's culture and reset the leadership climate to maintain standards, and the areas of mission clarity and connection will begin to turn around. All other organizational matters are and should be treated as secondary, at best, until this turnabout is made.

Cultural Resurgence

The FBI should take a hard look at the culture it currently promotes versus the culture it should have in its service to the American people. I long to see an assertive FBI return to a powerful sense of mission and a laser focus on operations that can re-instill an unshakeable confidence in the bureau's investigative conclusions. I would like to know that the bureau can be trusted once again to win the hard fights and bravely slay all of the monsters without becoming a monster itself. Maybe the FBI should look back to what it once was and seek a return to the professionalism and excellence that once defined it. Current members of the FBI who cannot or will not do this for the American people should be respectfully excused from FBI service.

I do not believe it is a question of how this transition can be done. I am confident that the FBI still has people in its ranks who know how to conduct investigations with the professionalism, objectivity, and skill that once made this organization the best. Where I have deep lingering concerns is in the willingness of our national leaders to seat a new cadre of dedicated leaders who will lead this effort. If our national leaders just pick more of the DC regulars to fill the FBI's key leadership roles, then nothing will change outside of cosmetic adjustments. Our national leaders must step away from the status quo and the old saying. "If you do what you have always done, you will get what you have always gotten." A new FBI leadership cadre must be united when advising the organization on what must be accomplished in line with expected outcomes. If these new bureau leaders need a place to start, they can go back to the discussions on what I was taught by my FBI mentors. They can also reference the File Review sections provided through Chapter 14 and the "New Rules to Live By." This change process will not be for faint-of-heart leaders but will require bold leaders who are dedicated to the success of the FBI and are unwavering in their beliefs. They must be steadfast in their desire to remake the FBI culture into one the American people can depend on, no matter the trials or tragedies that might be at hand.

I know these leaders still exist for this noble cause. Give them the chance to help.

Last Words

I struggled to find the right words to close this book. The right words that would summarize the attributes that the FBI could use in its self-assessment and effort to recover. I think I found the right words from Rudyard Kipling. The rendition below was given to me in framed artwork by a dear friend

Closing Thoughts

to commemorate my retirement from FBI service. These words say everything in the most eloquent way that I could not. While Kipling uses the following words to define what it means to be a man, I saw the adaptation of these words as providing a working standard that all FBI leaders, special agents, intelligence analysts, and professional staff members can aspire to in their service to the American people.

While I have struggled mightily and failed often to meet Kipling's aspirations, I continue to try every day. While hope is not a plan, I can only hope that the FBI I once knew can and will return to safeguard the security and welfare of our great nation.

If you can keep your head when all about you
Are losing theirs and blaming it on you;
If you can trust yourself when all men doubt you,
But make allowance for their doubting too;
If you can wait and not be tired by waiting,
Or, being lied about, don't deal in lies,
Or, being hated, don't give way to hating,
And yet don't look too good, nor talk too wise;

If you can dream—and not make dreams your master;
If you can think—and not make thoughts your aim;
If you can meet with triumph and disaster
And treat those two impostors just the same;
If you can bear to hear the truth you've spoken
Twisted by knaves to make a trap for fools,
Or watch the things you gave your life to, broken,
And stoop and build 'em up with worn-out tools:

Wanted: The FBI I Once Knew

If you can make one heap of all your winnings
And risk it on one turn of pitch-and-toss,
And lose, and start again at your beginnings
And never breathe a word about your loss;
If you can force your heart and nerve and sinew
To serve your turn long after they are gone,
And so hold on when there is nothing in you
Except the Will which says to them: "Hold on";

If you can talk with crowds and keep your virtue,
Or walk with kings—nor lose the common touch;
If neither foes nor loving friends can hurt you;
If all men count with you, but none too much;
If you can fill the unforgiving minute
With sixty seconds' worth of distance run—
Yours is the Earth and everything that's in it,
And—which is more—you'll be a Man, my son!

—Rudyard Kipling

www.ingramcontent.com/pod-product-compliance
Lightning Source LLC
Chambersburg PA
CBHW031424150426
43191CB00006B/383